MOTHERS OF
INCEST SURVIVORS

Mothers of Incest Survivors

ANOTHER SIDE OF THE STORY

Janis Tyler Johnson

Indiana University Press

BLOOMINGTON *&* INDIANAPOLIS

The paper used in this publication meets the minimum requirements of
American National Standard for Information Sciences—Permanence of Paper for
Printed Library Materials, ANSI Z39.48-1984.
∞™
Manufactured in the United States of America

Library of Congress Cataloging-in-Publications Data

Johnson, Janis Tyler.
    Mothers of incest survivors : another side of the story / Janis
Tyler Johnson.
        p. cm.
    Includes bibliographical references and index.
    ISBN 0-253-33096-3 (cl. : permanent paper). — ISBN 0-253-20737-1
(pa. : permanent paper)
        1. Incest victims—Family relationships—Case studies. 2. Mothers
    and daughters—Case studies. I. Title.
HQ71.J58 1992
306.877—dc20   91-46253
1 2 3 4 5   96 95 94 93 92

For the mothers who shared their stories so courageously and generously with me. Without their help, this book would never have been possible. Also, for mothers and daughters everywhere.

Contents

Preface

Over the past 15 years child sexual abuse and incest have become household words. What was once whispered about is now openly discussed in all levels of the media as well as in the family, schools, and churches. Today it has even passed its height as the issue of the hour and has settled down to be accepted as an almost commonplace occurrence. But it was not always so. During the latter part of the 1970s what was considered to be one of the "best kept secrets in the world"[1] began to spread to the general public through a proliferation of articles, radio and television programs, and personal accounts of survivors. One of the earliest accounts, *The Silent Sin*, is the story of a 17-year-old girl to her psychotherapist, billed as the "powerful personal story of a young girl's love affair with her father."[2] But it was not until *Ms.* published Ellen Weber's story, "Incest: Sexual Abuse Begins at Home," in 1977 that the secret really began to spread with such firsthand testimonials as Louise Armstrong's *Kiss Daddy Goodnight*; Charlotte Allen's *Daddy's Girl*; Katherine Brady's *Father's Days*; and Ellen Bass and Louise Thornton's collection of survivor stories, *I Never Told Anyone*.

As the statistics on the numbers of sexually abused children swelled 200% from 1972 to 1982,[3] it became apparent that what was once believed to be a powerful, universal prohibition[4] was apparently not working. And what Kinsey[5] had reported was not all that common had become, by 1984, a "hidden epidemic."[6] While the sex crimes against children had hit the front pages of newspapers in decades previous to the 1970s, there appears to be something different today about the way the public perceives and responds to the knowledge that large numbers of children are sexually misused and abused by adults.[7]

Why has the public become so openly and actively concerned with child sexual abuse and incest over the past 15 years? David Finkelhor suggests that child sexual abuse was discovered as a "'new' social problem" and emerged as a public issue in the mid-1970s with the rise of the child protection lobby, which connected child sexual abuse to the battered child syndrome, and the women's movement, which saw child sexual abuse as another manifestation of the general problem of rape.[8] Regardless of the reasons for alarm, the "Freudian cover-up"[9] that supported social denial for so long has been uncovered, and the public has ceased denying that adults sexually abuse children and that incest can and does happen. Diana Russell estimates that an estimated 4.5% of adult females have experienced an incestuous relationship with their fathers before the age of 18,[10] and David Finkelhor suggests that almost one-third of all child sexual abuse is committed by a family member.[11] This statistic will probably rise with new research on children who are coming forth to report their own sexual abuse while it is still going on.

While it was not always the case, most professionals now believe children who say they were sexually abused. The "incest hoax," a false report, may, in fact, be less common than the "false denial," the retraction of an incest report.[12] Yet, while child protective services, the police, and district attorneys are vigorously investigating and prosecuting child sexual abuse cases of all kinds, some, as reported by Russel Watson, are saying the "pendulum of enforcement has swung too far."[13] And a certain backlash against the veracity of children's reports is already being felt, particularly in child custody cases where mothers are accusing fathers.[14]

This book is about father-daughter incest. The concept "incest" holds different meanings for different groups historically and cross-culturally. Original meanings were not exclusively limited to sexual relations between people related by blood, they were also tied to the notion of kinship and ways of organizing marriage between people and groups. Currently, incest is associated more with the sexual behavior between adults and children than with marriage and kinship ties, but there has been an attempt by some to move away from the emotionally laden word "incest." David Finkelhor has pointed out that researchers and practitioners concerned about the sexual abuse of children have focused more narrowly on the sexual contacts between adults and children, and he argues against using the term "incest" since its broader meaning, rooted in the anthropological tradition, confuses the issue. He proposes instead the use of the term "family or intrafamilial sexual abuse."[15] However, while incest as sexual behavior is a unique form of child sexual abuse, people seem to feel differently about the sexual molestation of a child by a family member than by a stranger or a nonrelative. Emile Durkheim has written that incest holds and evokes a powerful sense of dread and horror because it violates the deeply held taboo of the blood tie.[16] For this reason, I have rejected the more inclusive term "child sexual abuse" in favor of the term "incest," precisely because it does tap feelings of dread and horror and thus holds a different level of meaning when applied to family sexual offenders. Another more important reason for using the term "incest" is because this is the term the mothers in this book used themselves.

There have been many books written about father-daughter incest, but what is new about this book is that it is written from the perspective of six mothers whose daughters were sexually abused by either their biological father or stepfather. It is a somewhat different story about what happens in the incest-family than has heretofore been told in the personal stories of adult survivors, the reports of clinicians, or the abstract formulations of theoreticians.

When daughters are sexually abused by a family member, which in most cases is a father or a father figure, it is generally the mother who is held liable. Thus, the same questions are asked over and over: "How could a mother let this happen? How could she not know? Why didn't she protect her daughter?" Up until now there has not been as much interest in studying the mothers of incest survivors[17] as there has been in studying survivors and offenders, so we really do not know how mothers would answer those questions.

In this book I set out to learn from the mothers themselves what the incest event was like for them, how they define and explain it, and what meaning the incest event holds for them. The result is another portrait of mothers of incest survivors, a portrait somewhat different from the collusive and powerless mothers who have dominated the literature on incest for so long. The self-reports of only six mothers are presented here, and their experiences cannot be generalized to other incest-family mothers. But their stories do open up the possibility that there may be yet more to learn about what happens within the incest-family than we have previously assumed.

My interest in incest began in the mid-1970s when, as a social worker with a public child welfare agency, I was responsible for developing a program to investigate referrals of suspected child abuse in compliance with the newly enacted Child Protective Services Law. This was my first experience with incest-families. My lack of knowledge, in the face of increasing numbers of incest referrals, sent me to the literature to learn more about and to gain some understanding of incest, a phenomenon I felt to be "beyond the pale." I wanted to find some guidelines to help me train workers to effectively respond to survivors and to develop intervention strategies that would be less traumatic for the incest-families we were serving than the incest event itself. At that time the "collusive mother" profile dominated the then sparse professional literature, yet some of the mothers I was seeing did not fit this model. As I listened to them I began to hear and understand their situation and behavior from a somewhat different perspective, and I had some hunches that things might not be quite what they seemed.

When I began my doctoral studies in the latter part of the 1970s I followed the increasing public interest in child sexual abuse and the accompanying media explosion. I continued to think about and study incest within the context of my general interest in families. When it came time for me to choose a dissertation topic, I decided to study mothers of incest survivors primarily because no one had yet studied them directly, but also because I was uncomfortable with the "mother-blaming" that pervaded the incest literature. At that time most information about mothers came from second- and thirdhand sources: the father, the daughter, or the professional working with either one. When researchers or clinicians did interview incest-family mothers, it was generally within the context of public institutional arrangements such as child welfare, criminal justice, and mental health systems. Under those circumstances, the mothers were "captive informants in a captive, alien environment,"[18] unlikely to let down their defenses against society's accusatory stance to say what they really thought and felt.

I began to wonder why there was so little interest in studying mothers while at the same time they were continually being seen as a vital source of protection for their daughters.[19] I wanted to learn directly from the mothers of incest survivors about their world from their point of view and to understand their feelings and their subjective reality. I believed that the assumptions held by the professional community[20] were not entirely well grounded because the information available about incest-family mothers simply did not tell the whole story, and that we would not have the whole story until we talked to the mothers themselves in a nonthreatening setting. I did not want to simply collect and report facts; I wanted to imagine their experiences behind the stories they would tell me.[21]

When I began this study, my primary goal was to learn from incest-family mothers and to understand the meanings of the events in their lives from their point of view. The reader who is interested in learning more about the process of locating the mothers, the interviews, and the methodological tools I used is directed to Appendix A: About the Study.

In chapter 1 I examine what the literature has had to say about incest-family mothers and their role in the family dynamics leading to incest. In chapter 2 I introduce the six mothers of incest victims who participated in this study. In chapters 3 through 7 the mothers speak for themselves around the themes I drew out of their stories. I discuss in chapter 8 what I learned from the mothers and offer, in chapter 9, some notes to professionals working with incest-families as well as to people who may know an incest-family mother. In the Epilogue I return to the mothers six years after interviewing them and after I had completed the manuscript for publication to see what had happened in their lives since we last spoke and to reflect on their lives and my experience with them.

Acknowledgments

This book began as my doctoral dissertation at the University of Pennsylvania School of Social Work. I was most fortunate that the members of my dissertation committee were willing to let me pursue an ethnographic study at a time when quantitative research was more highly valued and the methodology of choice. Peter Vaughan, Anne-Linda Furstenberg, Joseph Soffen, and Bambi Shieffelin supported and encouraged me to follow my own process. They were caring and critical; invested and available; and facilitated my work in a way that is congruent with the values and principles of social work practice.

Others contributed along the way. The administration at Immaculata College, where I teach, was most generous in providing me with both concrete and emotional support, including release time from teaching, funds to complete my research, and a sabbatical leave to revise the dissertation into a book. Friends and colleagues such as Barbara Simon, Patty Coleman, Marie Gatza, and Mary Lou Jewell encouraged me to follow my interest in incest-family mothers and to pursue this study because it was important, even if no one else was interested in studying mothers. The process from dissertation to book was a long one. Editors and readers along the road to publication offered support and astute comments. Some of these I followed, some I did not, so responsibility for the final product lies with me alone. To all of these people, I am grateful.

Finally, I want to thank my husband, Aaron, who believed I could do it, encouraged me to do it, and waited for and supported me in countless ways while I did do it.

MOTHERS OF
INCEST SURVIVORS

ONE

▬▬

Introduction

Almost every conceivable human woe—
autism, schizophrenia, psychosomatic
illness, psychopathologies of all kinds, you
name it—it is laid at some mother's feet.
It's all her fault. No matter what it is, if it
is serious and disturbing enough, cherchez
la mère. She is, according to one
psychiatrist, "pathogenic." She literally
breeds pathologies.
                    —Jessie Bernard, *Women, Wives,*
                                    and Mothers

Much has been written about incest from almost every perspective. From the beginning of recorded time incest and the taboo against it have been persistent, popular themes in mythology, scripture, literature, and drama.[1] Anthropology has pursued the questions surrounding the origin, function, persistence, and universality of the incest taboo.[2] Clinicians and researchers have studied everything, from the prevalence of incest, to the pathology and psychodynamics of the involved parties, to the initial and long-term effects on the survivors of incest.[3] When early incest studies could not agree on the personalities and pathology of fathers[4] or shed much light on the seduction of fathers by their daughters,[5] researchers began to realize that it was difficult to "capture the complexity of [incest] cases" when they focused only on individuals and their traits.[6] So, in the 1960s, spurred by the growing interest in family dynamics, researchers began to focus on the dynamics of the interpersonal relationships within the incest-family system. This meant moving beyond the father-daughter dyad to the father-daughter-mother triad, and in the process mothers of incest victims were indicted as the "key figure in the pathological family system."[7] This should not be so surprising since the portraits of mothers in incest families have simply conformed to the negative, mother-blaming attitudes that historically have been so prevalent in the literature and that are supported by those assumptions we continue to hold about the institution of motherhood.[8]

Certainly, the very secrecy of incest has made it difficult to design and carry out empirical studies grounded in sound methodological principles, and much of what has been said about mothers of incest survivors must be viewed skeptically.[9] But it is hard to know who the mothers of incest survivors really are when they have provided so little information about themselves. In many cases researchers and clinicians have not had easy access to incest-family mothers; in other cases they have ignored them; and in most cases, sexist assumptions about the roles of women in society and in the family have led to biased interpretations of their behavior.[10] The two interlocking pictures of incest-family mothers that prevail even today are the collusive mother, an "active nonparticipant" in the incestuous family affair, and the powerless mother, a childlike, helpless woman whose very powerlessness explains her collusion. Yet some clinicians are seeing and reporting that a protective mother does exist.[11]

Thus, three incest-family mother models prevail: the collusive mother, the powerless mother, and the shadowy, protective mother. Each is built on historical and cultural assumptions about mothers, and each is supported by its own underlying theoretical explanations.

The Collusive Mother

The collusive mother was born out of judgmental clinical statements made by male MDs,[12] that gained credence over time as each statement was footnoted by subsequent authors, all without any empirical referents. While Maurice Barry and Adelaide Johnson were the first to refer to the incest-family mother as "passively collusive" in print, they used the term more to explain the absence of visible signs of anxiety, fear, or guilt in the survivor of incest than to indict the mother. The mothers they described as "collusive" simply condoned the incest and turned the other way, but the word "collusive" to describe mothers became engraved in the incest literature.[13]

Since then, the collusive mother theme has changed and grown to encompass a mother who is a cold, frigid, withdrawn, physically ill, or psychologically impaired woman who resigns from her expected roles of responsible wife and mother and pushes her daughter into taking on her duties in the family, including satisfying the emotional and sexual needs of the father. The collusive mother avoids and denies the incest that goes on under her very nose. When confronted with its reality, she either disbelieves or blames her daughter. And following disclosure she chooses her husband over her daughter.[14] While clinicians and researchers have recognized that mothers have been studied much less than fathers or daughters, and that there may well be different existing profiles, the collusive mother is still preserved as authors continue to review and cite the literature that has fed and nurtured her.[15]

Psychoanalytic theory, with its emphasis on the unconscious forces within the individual and the Oedipal conflict, has provided one explanation for the collusive mother. According to this theory, incest-family mothers are symbiotically tied to their own depriving mothers and are eternally seeking love and approval only to be rejected and abandoned.[16] They relinquish their responsibilities as wives and mothers and push their daughters into assuming their roles in an attempt to become daughters again and recreate the opportunity to receive the love and support they never experienced with their own mothers. Incest-family mothers have never resolved their own Oedipal fantasies, perceive their daughters as the replica of a rejecting maternal grandmother, and displace all the hostility they really felt for their own mothers onto their daughters. It is this mother-daughter hostility, passed down from one generation to the next, that is said to explain the estrangement between mothers and daughters[17] and the inability of mothers to act as crucial controlling agents in the incest-affairs.[18]

In contrast to the psychoanalytic perspective, a family systems approach looks at the interrelatedness of family members and concludes that all family members actually participate in the "family affair," including even the nonparticipating parent, the mother.[19] The incest-family mother is said to collude out of her absence or incapacity and her sexual rejection of her husband, all of which lead to role reversal with her daughter and ultimately to the incest event. Thus, we have the definitive colluding mother who abandoned her wife and mother roles to become the "cornerstone in the pathological family system."[20]

From this redundant profile of the incest-family mother we arrive at two major themes that underlie her collusion: her sexual rejection of her husband and her role reversal with her daughter. Tamar Cohen aptly captures these themes as she "revisits" the incestuous family:

> Two specific components in the behavior of the mother have been observed as important to the understanding of incest: her abdication of her role as a mother and housewife while delegating those responsibilities to her daughter, and her backing out of her sexual role as a wife. These characteristics appear in nearly all mothers of the classic incestuous families.[21]

The Powerless Mother

Many of the same clinicians and researchers who saw the collusive mother recognized her powerlessness in the "overwhelmingly patriarchal" incest-family.[22] Incest survivors themselves have portrayed their fathers as more powerful than their mothers, whom they described as helpless, defeated, victimized, and powerless, unable to protect themselves, much less their daughters.[23] And it is only recently that incest has been placed within the context of a pattern of family violence,[24] despite the fact that the physical abuse of incest-family mothers has been documented since 1968.[25] Judith Herman has suggested that it was the mother's very powerlessness that explained and measured her collusion.[26] Yet this picture of the powerless mother was seldom included in subsequent reviews of the literature and has generally been buried under descriptions of the collusive mother, the one most often seen and studied.[27]

A feminist perspective that moved beyond the individual-level analysis soon emerged, locating the incest taboo and its violations within the structure of patriarchy and male dominance and supremacy. Judith Herman and Lisa Hirschman set father-daughter incest within the patriarchal family.[28] Sandra Butler saw mothers of incest survivors "scrutinized, blamed, and ultimately impaled on the sword of male-dominated analysis"[29] and called for a different kind of analysis to find out how they became that way.

As feminists began to see incest more as an issue of power than sex, they rejected the collusive mother paradigm to promote a feminist analysis of the existence and impact of patriarchy on the behavior of mothers. They pointed to and identified the rules a woman must learn to become a proper wife and mother; the father's role in the process of the mother-daughter estrangement and the subsequent mother-daughter role reversal; and the connection between the incest event and the patriarchal society and culture within which it occurs.[30]

Feminist writers pointed out that wives who had been socialized to traditional female sex roles had been conditioned into a state of helplessness and lacked the personal, economic, and social resources to assume the assertive roles necessary to protect their daughters. They also taught their daughters what it meant to be female. And even if they did not intend to do so, they taught their daughters what they could expect from their fathers and how they should behave in the family. Adrienne Rich universalizes the handing down of the victim role from one generation to another:

> A mother's victimization does not merely humiliate her, it mutilates the daughter who watches her for clues as to what it means to be a woman. Like the traditional foot-bound Chinese woman, she passes on her own affliction.[31]

In the case of the incest-family, the mother passed on not only her female roles but her sense of powerlessness as well. Some view the incest-family mother to be as much a victim as her daughter.[32] According to the feminist perspective it is not the collusive mother but "male supremacy [that] is the cornerstone of the pathological family system."[33]

The Protective Mother

There is a protective mother in the incest literature, but we do not really have a very sharp picture of her. This may be due to the lack of a clear conceptualization of what we mean by "protective." Do we mean a mother's protection of her daughter *from* incest or protection of her daughter *following* the disclosure of incest? In post-disclosure protection there are a number of different actions a mother can take, but there is not always agreement on what kind of action constitutes protection of the daughter, or what the daughter is being protected against.

Kirson Weinberg identified a number of different behaviors among incest-family mothers following the disclosure of incest. The collusive mothers tolerated the incest affair, condoned the father's behavior, sanctioned social suppression, and did nothing to protect their daughters. Other mothers protected their daughters by removing them from the home while they remained with their husbands. A third group were hostile to their husbands and actively protected their daughters, drawing the battle lines between the family and the father. Weinberg concluded that the patriarchal organization of the family and the father's dominance and intimidation of family members made it unlikely that very many mothers would be able to behave in such a powerful, protective way.[34]

Why are some mothers able to protect their daughters following disclosure? Some possible answers include: they were ready to leave the marriage anyway and the incest provided the final stimulus to do so;[35] the mother had alternative resources and support available outside the marriage to help her to sustain any protective action she initiated;[36] and the mother's empathy toward her daughter and her anger toward her husband were stronger than her need for him, whether that need be one of love and affection or out of economic dependence.[37]

While others have studied the factors related to maternal protectiveness,[38] only Margaret Myer has directly addressed and gathered information on the ability of incest-family mothers, from their own self-reports and clinical assessments of them, to protect their daughters following disclosure of the incest. Myer categorized 43 mothers drawn from a study population of sexually abused children and their families into three groups: (1) protective mothers, who protected their daughters and rejected their mates; (2) immobilized mothers, who did nothing; and (3) rejecting mothers, who rejected their daughters and protected their mates. While 24 (over half) of the mothers Myer studied took protective action following disclosure, they were all characterized as extremely passive, dependent personalities. Thus, their potential to initiate and carry through with any protective action had to be attributed to something that superseded their dependence and passivity.

Even while there are reports that some mothers do act protectively, it has been difficult for those working with incest-families to give up their belief in the "collusive mother." A summary of Myer's study of mothers appeared in the March 1984 issue of *NASW News*[39] and elicited a response that took issue with Myer's findings of protective incest-family mothers:

> To turn a blind eye to the role of the mother . . . turns away from what is known about family systems as well as what is known about object relationships and the role of the unconscious in playing out past traumas in

current reality. There is no empirical reason to think that such a destructive event as incest could occur in the family relationship field independent of any contribution on the part of the mother, whether conscious or unconscious, active or passive.[40]

And with this we have come full circle, back to the collusive incest-family mother.

This study of mothers of incest survivors is quite different from the studies previously cited. I did not set out to challenge or support any of the above models, or to test any hypotheses, but to discover from the mothers themselves what the incest event has been like for them. What I learned from them broadened considerably my own ideas about what happens in an incest family and went far beyond anything the literature has had to say about mothers to date.

I hope this book will do two things. First, it is intended to modify some of the assumptions about incest-family mothers that are held by professionals who work with incest families, assumptions that often give rise to more anger toward the mother who did not protect her daughter from incest than toward the father who actually committed the incest.[41] This anger limits the professional's potential to develop a helping relationship with mothers of incest survivors, interferes with comprehensive, realistic investigations and assessment of alleged incest, and precludes effectively helping incest-families following disclosure. Currently held assumptions and available information about incest-family mothers do not tell the whole story. This book adds another piece to that story, a piece that proposes, like Myer,[42] that not only are mothers of incest victims not all alike, but that they and their lives are much more complicated than current theories suggest.

But there is a second, even more persuasive reason for telling the stories of the mothers in this book, and that is to help other mothers who may suspect or know that their daughters are now being or were sexually abused by a family member. There is little in the media or literature to give them a sense that they are not alone; that other mothers share their experience; that we should pay attention and listen to them as well as to victims and sexual offenders. Diane, one of the mothers in this book, said it well:

> For one thing, there is no information to help mothers. I've tried to get information. Most of it is very technical though and not in a language most mothers could understand. Mostly there was nothing that could give me comfort at a very trying time.

Now it is time to meet the mothers in this book and to hear their stories.

TWO

—

Meet the Mothers

Originally, I wanted to locate 20 incest-family mothers who would be willing to speak with me about their experiences. This proved to be a more formidable task than I expected. In over a year and a half, only six mothers came forth as a result of the different strategies I used to locate them.[1] This emphasizes the difficulty in finding mothers to study and may well explain why there has been so little research on them in the past. Unlike daughters and fathers in incest-families, mothers are for the most part outside the jurisdiction of professionals with authority. Daughters come under the protective umbrellas of child welfare services, mental health agencies, and the legal system. Fathers come under the social control of the criminal justice and judicial systems. But mothers are usually on the perimeter of these systems, and in most cases defensively so, which makes it doubly difficult for researchers and clinicians to gain their trust and to have open, genuine contact with them.

I have made every effort to protect the privacy and identities of the mothers in this book, and in so doing I have changed a number of details about them and their families. But at the same time I have also tried to characterize them as faithfully as possible and to preserve the essence of their lives and situations.

As I introduce you to the mothers I will tell you how we met, where they were in their own lives at that point in time, and the reasons they gave for being willing to tell me about the incest in their families from their perspectives. I will tell you something about their family backgrounds, how they presented themselves, how I experienced them, and what is going on in their lives at the present time, six years after the completion of the interviews. Then I will summarize some of the commonalities they shared and the variations they exhibited to illustrate how, although they shared a common world with each other, they also differed from each other in a number of ways.

Ann

I met Ann, nearing 60, through her 27-year-old daughter, whom I had known as an adult survivor of incest. Ann was in a crisis when we first met. She had just separated from her husband of over 35 years after learning that he had sexually abused their teenage granddaughter, had left her home and all her possessions, and was living temporarily with a friend. At this time she had just learned that her husband had also sexually abused their two daughters over a period of time some 20 years earlier. Professional authorities became involved around the grandfather-granddaughter incest. Ann's husband was criminally charged and at the time we met he was participating in a sexual offender program.

Although a shy, private woman, Ann was willing to speak with me, with the support of her daughter, because she needed to talk to someone about what she had just learned and to understand for herself what had happened. And out of her own history of having had no one to turn to, Ann also had a strong desire to help other incest-family mothers to deal more effectively with incest if it occurred in their families.

Ann came from a traditional, middle-class family background.[2] Following graduation from high school she worked as a sales clerk and lived at home until she married, at age 19, a college-educated, professional man. She described herself as very young and naive in sexual knowledge and experience and their courtship and early marriage as quite ordinary except for the conflict she experienced between her religion and the use of birth control. Ann presented herself as a typical, middle-class, suburban housewife and mother of four children of the post-World War II "professional homemaker" generation. She never worked outside the home after marriage, but while her children were growing up she was active in community activities that were child related. To many of their friends, Ann and her husband were an "ideal couple."

A crisis occurred in the family during the twelfth year of marriage when Ann discovered, quite by accident, that her husband had been "touching" their oldest daughter, then 10 years old. She confronted her husband but he talked her out of doing anything about it. He convinced her she was overreacting.

Ann always came to our meetings fastidiously dressed and groomed. She presented herself as a rather passive but gentle, caring woman behind a screen of fragility, stepping out occasionally to reveal an inner strength, which she was slowly experiencing along with her growing awareness of a new reality. She talked slowly and thoughtfully, searching for just the right word to ensure that she was being meticulously fair. Long pauses punctuated her story as she tried to reveal things she had never talked about before and to speak about the unspeakable. Ann was the first mother I interviewed. In my own urgency to learn how incest-family mothers viewed and experienced the incest event, it was difficult for me at first to listen patiently, as she told her story in her own way and in her own time. Soon I learned to follow her slow but thoughtful rhythm.

During the time Ann spoke with me, she made tremendous strides in her own personal growth. She entered therapy, obtained a legal separation from her husband, began taking courses at a nearby community college, and started working part time.

Ann's life is very different today, "so turned around from what it was." She has divorced her husband and has absolutely no contact with him, but she does see her children and grandchildren regularly. She works as a secretary in a women's center, a very positive, comfortable setting for her. She enjoys her contact with women who are making changes in their lives and likes using herself and her own experiences to help other women. Ann lives alone in a small apartment with her cat.

Ann participated in 17 separate interviews in my office. The interviews lasted from two to three hours each for a total of 39 hours of interview time.

Bonnie

Bonnie, in her early thirties, learned of my study through a friend who had picked up a letter I had addressed to incest-family mothers and distributed throughout the community. When we met, Bonnie was a partner in an investment firm where she began as a clerk-typist. She had been divorced from her second husband for several years, was living alone with her teenage daughter by her first husband and two younger sons by her second husband, and was engaged in a series of court hearings around custody and her ex-husband's visitation rights with his sons.

Bonnie was eager to talk with me since she was planning to write her own story and I had "come along at just the right time." Bonnie wanted to sort out her own role in the incest event and to satisfy any guilty feelings she had about what happened between her daughter, then age 14, and her stepfather.

Bonnie came from an "old" upper middle-class, professional family background. Her plans to attend college were interrupted when she became pregnant in her senior year in high school. She married her boyfriend after graduation and gave birth to their daughter several months later. The marriage ended after three years, and almost immediately following the divorce Bonnie married an older man of some authority in the community. She saw in him her "guardian angel, a protector, a father" who would take care of her and "save her from all the world." "I was never going to have to grow up," was the way Bonnie put it. Her husband proved to be an unstable alcoholic and a "dominating monster" whom she divorced seven years later when he began to physically abuse their oldest son.

Bonnie learned of the incest from her daughter a year following the divorce, which was a year and a half before she began to meet with me. The incest started when her daughter was four years old, at a time of multiple family crises and losses, and lasted until the divorce six years later. Bonnie later learned that her husband had also sexually abused her younger cousin, and there was some suspicion that he had molested a niece before his marriage to Bonnie. The incest was never reported; Bonnie never confronted her ex-husband with her knowledge;

and no outside, professional authorities were ever involved with the family.

Bonnie, a tiny, delicate woman, usually wore her businesswoman suits and carried a briefcase almost as big as herself. When she was not "dressed for success," she wore the casual garb of a teenager. Bonnie presented herself with a forceful strength, although the little girl in her was always peeping out around the corner. She was compelled to tell her story and talked in a rapid staccato, seldom completing a sentence, as if her thoughts had raced ahead of her ability to form words. In contrast to my experience with Ann, I sometimes found it difficult to keep up with Bonnie. She was a generous, free-flowing informant who became interested in and involved with my study as a whole, not just her own piece in it. She was bright and enthusiastic, with a high level of energy, and was more a collaborating partner than a subject to be studied.

At the present time Bonnie is still single and has no wish to remarry. She is more content, calmer, and says she is not fighting as many battles. She looks more grown up—more mature beyond being six years older. Bonnie is still a successful career woman but tries to balance her business life with a committed investment in the lives and activities of her three children. Her daughter is now a student at college.

Bonnie participated in seven separate interviews in my office, each interview lasting from one and a half to three hours for a total of 17 hours of interview time.

Cathy

Cathy, in her mid-thirties, was referred to me by her social worker. Cathy had learned of the incest a year earlier (to the day of our first interview) when the police came to their home and arrested her husband after her daughter had reported the incest to them. Her husband did not deny the charges. Cathy was unclear about when the incest began or how long it had continued, but she dated it to when her daughter was approximately age 11 and thought it continued for about two years. At the time of the interviews Cathy's husband was serving a prison sentence for incest with the oldest of their four daughters.

Cathy was motivated and agreed to talk with me in order to understand what had happened in her family for incest to have occurred. She also believed her own story would help other mothers.

Cathy came from what she described as a caring, traditional, working-class family background and married her high school boyfriend at age 16 when she became pregnant, an event they had both planned. Her husband left immediately following the "secret" wedding their parents had arranged for a job-training program in another state, and she joined him six months after their daughter was born. Within the next five years three more daughters and a son were born. Cathy remembered and described their early marriage as good years. They were marred only by her husband's extramarital affair, which occurred during a period when she was sexually unavailable because of severe physical problems following the birth of their third daughter, and his escalating drinking, which contributed to his erratic, unpredictable behavior and bursts of anger.

Cathy went as far as the tenth grade in high school, leaving school when she became pregnant, and had worked off and on as a clerk in small shops after all her children were in school. At the time of the interviews she was unemployed, receiving public assistance, and enrolled in a WIN program to become a child care worker. Cathy was planning to reconcile with her husband upon his release from prison on the conditions that he not take another drink and was willing to work on "getting the family back to normal."

Cathy was always well groomed, with a well-scrubbed look, when she came to talk with me. She moved slowly and carried herself with dignity. She had a warm smile and her large, expressive, dark eyes always kept steady contact with mine as we talked. Cathy spoke slowly and softly, telling her story in a deliberate, orderly way, a gentle humor underlying her words. She was unusually straightforward and answered all questions without any evasion. Although Cathy described herself as a private, shy person, she spoke freely to me from the very beginning, expressing a range of emotions from teary sadness to anger tempered with a stubborn determination. She exhibited a kind of common-sense sensibility grounded in a strong value and belief system from which she would not waiver. Cathy tended to see the world in concrete terms, as black or white, good or bad, right or wrong. She exuded a quiet strength, courage, and self-reliance mixed with a tinge of little-girl helplessness.

Cathy and her husband are living together today after a four-year separation. Her husband served two years in prison and lived apart from the family for two years, as a condition of his parole, until his youngest daughter graduated from high school and left home. Cathy describes life as a lot better today. Her husband has not picked up a drink since the day he was arrested, and she describes things as being the way they were when they were first married. Cathy has frequent, regular contact with all her children, who live nearby, and describes her relationship with her daughter, now married, as "still close."

I talked with Cathy on five separate occasions in my motel room, each interview lasting from one and a half to three and a half hours for a total of thirteen and a half hours of interview time.

Diane

Diane, in her mid-forties, was also referred to me by her social worker. A year earlier she had become suspicious that her husband was sexually abusing their 13-year-old daughter. With the support and encouragement of her therapist, Diane reported the incest to the authorities. Her husband denied the incest allegation and Diane then forced him to leave the home with a Protection from Abuse Order. She was considering a reconciliation when the order would be up in a few months.

Diane was willing to talk with me because she believed her own story would help and give comfort to other mothers in the same situation as hers.

Diane came from a traditional, blue-collar family background where incest was an intergenerational theme. She had been sexually abused by an uncle and an older brother, and 14 years earlier her husband had molested their oldest daughter when she was nine years old. Diane had confronted her husband on that occasion without involving outsiders, and she believed she had stopped the incest from continuing. A third daughter had been sexually molested by a family friend.

Diane married at age 17 because her husband, whom she had just met, "thought they should." She was being sexually abused by her uncle at the time and saw marriage as one way to escape that situation. She had seven children, three daughters and four sons, within 12 years, although there was barely a year between the births of the first four children.

I interviewed Diane in her own home. We sat at a heavy, round table covered with a lace tablecloth in her large, homey, immaculate kitchen. She expressed real pride in her beautiful Cape Cod-style home, which she and her husband had "built with their own hands." Despite her social worker's caution that she might be somewhat reticent about speaking freely with me, Diane described her experience almost nonstop with a heavy, steady, sadness in her voice, emphasizing significant, key words as if to underline the seriousness of her story. I felt like a listening wall and said almost nothing during the first hour. It was not necessary to ask questions to keep Diane talking. It was an intense, somewhat tearful interview with this woman, whose history of losses and depression still seemed to weigh her down, but who was now struggling to grow and meet her own needs in new ways.

Today Diane is reconciled with her husband. They bought a small business together and Diane keeps the books, working part time as a bookkeeper for another small business as well. She describes her relationship with her husband as much better now, because she doesn't let him push her around. Diane states that she doesn't let things happen that she does not want to happen, and she feels she has much more control over her own life. Diane has forgiven her husband but never forgets. "I have a granddaughter and we all keep an eye on things—we never let our guard down." Diane's daughter is now in her early twenties, works full time, and still lives at home.

I interviewed Diane once for two and a half hours.

Ellen

Ellen, in her late thirties, called me when she read about my study in a local newspaper article. She was motivated to talk with me in order to let people understand "how these things start" and "how a person feels" as well as to "stop this from happening to other chidren."

Ellen came from a chaotic, violent, working-class family that was well known to community social service agencies. She had been sexually abused by her two older brothers when she was approximately four years old. She first married at age 16 to the "first guy who had me" figuring "no one else would want me after him." They separated shortly before their son was born. Believing her marriage had been annulled, Ellen married again at age 19 because she was lonely and found it hard to be on her own with a small child. A daughter was born to this marriage, which Ellen described as violent, with chronic separations and "running around" on both sides. Ellen and her second husband finally separated permanently after 11 years of marriage, at which time their daughter, then age 10, decided to live with her father rather than with Ellen. After she was divorced, Ellen married a third time.

Ellen had learned of the incest a year before our interview from child welfare authorities in the county where her ex-husband and daughter were living. Her daughter reported the incest had lasted from the time she was three until she was 15 years old. The father was charged but was not convicted because of a legal technicality.

Like Diane, Ellen talked with me in her home, a well-kept, attractive rancher with marigolds flanking the walk to the front door. Inside everything was immaculate, polished, and orderly. Photographs of family members along with wedding pictures of Ellen and her present husband lined the walls. Pictures of Ellen showed a well-groomed, attractively made-up woman who resembled a popular country music star. We always sat at her kitchen table, where we both drank the coffee she automatically made for my arrival. Ellen smoked steadily, filling an empty ashtray with half-smoked cigarettes before we finished talking. During our interviews she was usually suffering from sinus and migraine headaches and often looked tired from the pain, her eyes red and teary.

Ellen talked steadily, remembering the dates of births, marriages, separations, divorces, and remarriages with remarkable accuracy. She presented a detailed, chronological overview of the events in her life with little difficulty. Her voice was tinged with a nervous shrillness backed by laughter turned against herself. Ellen was candidly honest, revealing all, withholding nothing, and I had no sense that she was trying to present me with a one-sided version of her experience. She told it like it was and did not attempt to make herself look good and others bad, admitting her own limitations without being unrealistically hard on herself. She thoughtfully answered all my questions, often pausing to think before speaking. Like the other mothers I interviewed before her, Ellen was willing to risk the pain of telling her story in order to share her experience with me.

Ellen is still happily married to her third husband. Her physical health is much better; she has stopped smoking, and she sounds calmer, less hysterical. Overall, her relationship with her daughter is better; they are talking more now, "woman to woman." But Ellen still struggles with the old theme of being "outside" since her daughter has chosen to have contact with her father. The feeling of being in "limbo" is still there. Her daughter is married and has a daughter of her own. Ellen cannot forgive her ex-husband for what he did, not only to their daughter, but to her, and she fears he will abuse their granddaughter.

I met with Ellen five times. The interviews lasted from two to three hours each for a total of 12 hours of interview time.

Fay

Fay, in her late twenties, was referred to me by an attorney to whom she had gone for legal advice about divorcing her husband. I interviewed her in my office within 24 hours of the time she discovered the incest between her 11-year-old daughter and her second husband. Fay was willing to talk with me to help other mothers and for her own need to talk to "see the overall picture and where I went wrong."

Fay came from a blue-collar, working-class background and a family where her alcoholic father physically abused her mother and the children. She went as far as the tenth grade in high school, and later earned her Graduate Equivalency Diploma. Fay was 18 when she gave birth to her daughter out of wedlock. Three years later she married but divorced her husband after a year. She married her present husband, the incest offender, two years after her divorce, because she was pregnant. She claimed she would never have married him otherwise. Fay described the marriage as one crisis after another. Her husband was a compulsive drinker and gambler, had been on probation for theft, had gone bankrupt, and was violent when he had been drinking.

At the time of the interview Fay had pressed charges against her husband for incest and he was out of jail on bail awaiting a preliminary hearing. She had filed for divorce and was getting ready to move back to her home state within the week to live temporarily with her mother.

Fay is a slim, well-groomed young woman. She presented herself in a controlled, calm manner, speaking softly and articulately with a steely seriousness that belied the emotional feelings that seeped through as she recounted what had happened to her daughter and what she was going to do about it. Her large, blue eyes looked at me steadily as she spoke. She was very open in sharing information about herself and her life, and

no topic was too painful fo her to delve into. Fay credited the Lord with
guiding and supporting her through everything she and her daughter had
endured. She impressed me as a strong, decisive, active woman who had
no ambivalence about what she had to do to protect her daughter.

At the present time, six years later, Fay is "happily" remarried and
living in her home state. She returned to college and earned a degree in
accounting and currently works as an accountant in a department store.
Her daughter is now a teenager and is doing relatively well in all areas,
although Fay is still concerned about what her daughter will do if she
gives her too much freedom. Both Fay and her daughter received counseling following disclosure. Fay's ex-husband pleaded guilty to the incest
charges and is currently serving a prison sentence.

I interviewed Fay once, for two and a half hours.

Commonalities

Adrienne Rich has written, "Women have both had and not had a common world."[3] And so it was with the women in this study. The mothers
shared the traditional world of women before they came to the research
situation. They all began their marriages young (the average age was 19),
and all, except Fay, were sexually naive, uninformed, and inexperienced
when they first married. They were all economically dependent upon
their husbands and in some cases emotionally and socially dependent
as well. They all came from traditional families of origin where the
models of male-female and husband-wife hierarchical relationships reinforced and supported their economic dependency. Mothers stayed home,
and if they had ever worked, they returned to the home after marrying,
and those who returned to work outside the home usually encountered
a great deal of resistance from their husbands.

Their worlds did change after the disclosure of the incest event, and
on this point the mothers in this study share other common, significant
experiences. Their worlds were split open at the time of the disclosure,
the foundations of their lives were shaken, their families were shattered.
Their daughters had been robbed of their childhoods and the mothers were
left feeling hurt and betrayed by their husbands. But the crisis at the time
of disclosure provided new opportunities to see their lives and worlds
differently, to make new decisions, and to solve old problems in new ways.

During the interviews the mothers were similar in other ways. All
were eager and impatient to talk about themselves, about their experiences and lives, and, most importantly, about their feelings. They demonstrated little interest in the explanations I presented during the first
interview about myself, the study, or the protective guidelines for the
interview process. All the mothers were verbally articulate, spoke freely
without interruption, and, with the exception of Ann, required minimal
encouragement, questioning, or probing from me.

All the mothers conveyed that no one had ever expressed an interest in them or their feelings about the incest event before. If the secret had been revealed to outsiders, the professionals involved had focused on their daughters and husbands, leaving them alone with their feelings. They all said it was my genuine interest in them that made it easy to talk with me. They desperately wanted to sort things out for themselves, to understand better what had happened to them and their daughters and their families; but they also wanted to help other mothers in the same situation. All the mothers expressed their need to talk about their feelings, not only about the incest, but about other aspects of their lives, both before and after the incest event. Bonnie said it well; she had not always been an incest-mother and she wanted to understand how she got there. She also believed there was a life before and after the incest, meaning that not all the things that happened in her family before the incest event necessarily contributed to it nor that all the things that happened afterward were necessarily consequences of it.

One theme dominated the stories the mothers told: their marital relationships. And it was to this theme that they repeatedly returned as they told their stories. All the mothers believed they had been victimized, punished, and hurt by their husbands as much as their daughters had been, if not more so. This common sense of victimization, while directed to their feelings about the incest event, cut across a wide range of other life issues as they discussed their relationships with their husbands.

As the interviews progressed the mothers became very involved in the study. They became interested in the progress of the work, and all read, commented on, and approved, as accurately representing their experiences, feelings, and meanings, both this chapter and the chapters that tell their stories.

The mothers shared one last commonality: they were all very likable. I was impressed with their strength, their willingness to open up the pain in their lives and to relive and endure it while they told me their stories. This is in contrast to an impression gained from the literature and professionals working with incest-family mothers, which is that they are cold, detached, unfeeling, and uncaring.

Variations

While the six mothers shared many commonalities, they also demonstrated a wide range of variability. They all wanted to claim their uniqueness as individuals and to see themselves as different from other incest-family mothers.[4] And they were different from each other in the details of their family and socioeconomic backgrounds, marital and family experiences, the circumstances surrounding the disclosure of the incest, their responses to the disclosure, their explanations for why the incest happened in their family, and the meaning the incest event held for each of them. The variability found among the six mothers in this study suggests a wider range of possible differences among the mothers of incest victims who come to the attention of the authorities and supports Margaret Myer's conclusion that not all incest mothers are alike.[5]

During the process of the interviews each mother focused on and emphasized different areas and events in her life. Together their stories wove a tapestry of themes made up of a variety of patterns and textures. It was almost as if there were many yarns of different fibers, thicknesses, and colors, each mother choosing sometimes the same and at other times different strands of yarn from the other mothers—each weaving in her own way her own unique design into the overall pattern of the tapestry.

The mothers began their stories somewhat differently. Bonnie, Cathy, and Fay began with the night they found out and the circumstances of discovery. Diane started with her experience of finding no information to help her, nothing to give her "comfort at a very trying time." Ellen began with her own "rotten childhood" and sexual abuse. Ann needed to talk about the more positive aspects of her husband, family, and life before she could even begin to approach the incest material.

In the following five chapters the reader has the opportunity to listen to the mothers share their experiences. I have organized their stories around the themes I extracted from their individual stories. While this format makes it somewhat difficult for the reader to follow the course of each mother's experience sequentially, I have chosen this structure for the higher value of protecting the identities and privacy of the mothers who made this book possible.

THREE

The Secret Is Revealed

You wonder how it can go on for so many
people and nobody says nothing.
(Diane)

For many families the conspiracy of silence may last for generations,
providing a pseudo-safety net that entangles the family into a self-made
prison. Today this web of silence is breaking as more victims and family
members are willing to name and reveal the secret. In this chapter the
mothers will talk about how they discovered the incest, their previous
knowledge of it, and how they initially responded.

Disclosure

Let me tell you about the night I found
out.
(Bonnie)

Disclosure of the incest event was a significant marker and separated
the worlds the mothers experienced before the revelation of the incest
from the worlds they experienced after it was disclosed. The world before
was not necessarily better or happier, and family life was usually dys-
functional and fraught with problems, but the disclosure highlighted
those problems and provided an opportunity for the mothers to confront
and solve old problems in new ways.

Incest is disclosed in two ways, accidentally and purposefully.[1] Accidental disclosure includes discovery, either of the incest behavior itself
or clues leading to the knowledge of it. The secret is revealed accidentally
when no one intended to tell. In purposeful disclosure a participant in
the incest event decides to tell an outsider who might or might not be
the mother, but which usually leads to her finding out.

Accidental or purposeful dimensions of disclosure were not as critical
for the mothers I spoke with as the dimensions of private or public
disclosure, for, as we shall see, private disclosure still keeps the incest
a secret within the family, and nothing changes. Three mothers accidentally discovered the sexual behavior between their husbands and

daughters, and for two of them the disclosure was kept a private matter within the family.

Diane described how she fell asleep in the living room and accidentally discovered her husband molesting her oldest daughter, then age nine:

> The kitchen table was visible from the davenport, and I woke up, and he was setting there with her on his lap, and he was fondling her breast. She was nine or ten at the time.

Diane told me she felt adequate at that time to deal with her husband alone, and she was satisfied that her confrontation with him then put an end to any further sexual behavior between him and her daughter:

> I sent her to bed and then I talked to him. I told him I didn't want it to happen again, or he would be out. I didn't go to any officials. It was strictly between us.

Ann, too, accidentally discovered the incest when her seven-year-old daughter cried out in the middle of the night. "Daddy" had come into her room and, mistaking her for her older sister in whose bed she was sleeping, "tried to do something to her." Her older sister then revealed that daddy had been "doing things to her."

Ann's experience was different from Diane's when she confronted her husband. He used his position of authority and power in the family to intimidate her to support his own denial and to suppress any further disclosure of the incest event. Ann sat in her "ladylike" posture, hands in her lap, ankles crossed, only her voice belying the confusion she still felt as she explained:

> This is stupid, but I didn't know what incest was. I had never heard of anything like this, but I had a sense that it was wrong because of my reaction—something inside of me just absolutely turned over. I felt like I was in a totally different zone. I had just heard something that shook the whole foundation of my life. But you see, I was talked down by my husband. I thought that my knowledge and perception of what happened was probably lopsided. That was always my fear—that I overreacted, was too emotional one way or the other. And I really did explode all over. I was going to call the police and everything. I just went off my gourd about it. And my husband said nothing serious happened, it really wasn't anything, and I had overreacted because I didn't understand. He said others wouldn't believe it and this was just a lot of fuss about nothing and that it wouldn't be understood and would break up the family, or maybe that they'd take the children away from me or something. And I did calm down, reasoning with myself that I was overreacting.

Both Ann and Diane discovered the incest accidentally and confronted their husbands privately without any support, assistance, or direction from outsiders, and both fathers went on to sexually abuse other children in the family.

For Fay, the circumstances surrounding accidental disclosure were somewhat different. Still breathless, only 24 hours after her discovery, Fay sat on the edge of the chair in my office and recited, in a controlled, soft voice, what had happened:

> My daughter's eleven-year-old friend spent the night. I had to work that night and, when I got home about ten or eleven, my husband was up, and he said that he had to tell me something—that he had tried something with my daughter's friend, sexually, and she was going to tell her mother. He was really upset about this because he was afraid. . . . I talked to the child and the next day called her mother and told her what had happened. Now, I had no idea that anything had happened with my daughter at this point, but I just had a sneaky suspicion, so I went to my daughter and asked her, "How many times has your dad touched you?" just assuming that I knew. She said, "A couple," but I knew something more had happened; she was afraid and overly reserved.

Fay learned from her daughter the details of the incest and, instead of confronting her husband directly, went immediately to the authorities to press charges against him, making the disclosure public and getting support to take further action.

Four survivors purposefully revealed the incest. Ann's granddaughter disclosed during a family therapy session that her grandfather had sexually abused her, which resulted in a report by the family therapist to the authorities. It was then that Ann learned that her husband had continued to abuse her two daughters after she had confronted him many years earlier.

Bonnie had been divorced for a year before her daughter told her about the incest. She recounted how her daughter had been acting "crazy" every time she went out at night, which led to her finding out about the incest:

> I got this phone call at work right after school and she was crying hysterically. "You're not going out tonight are you? Don't go out. Don't leave me alone." So I went home and said, "I don't know what's bothering you, but we've got to talk and resolve this." And she started crying, and I remember putting my arm around her and her just sobbing on my shoulder, and I said, "What's wrong?" and she said, "I can't tell you, you'll get mad." And then she said, "It's dad." Then the light bulbs went off, and I said, "Was he touching you?" and she said, "Yes."

Bonnie learned this a year after the incest had ceased. Bonnie never confonted him about the incest, nor were any people outside the family involved. When I asked Bonnie about this she said she would never have reported it nor would she have involved the police, "Because I am very realistic about the support I would get from society."

Two daughters purposefully told authorities outside the family. Cathy's daughter told the police, who then came to the home to arrest her husband. Cathy's voice was steady and quiet, breaking occasionally with the remembered shock as she told me about that night:

> She hadn't told anybody about it before. They [the authorities] said she had been talking to her boyfriend and that she was crying and upset, and I guess her and her father had a fight or something and her boyfriend said, "Has he hurt you?" and then she started telling him all about all this. She had never talked to anybody about it; she kept it inside and then she had somebody to talk to and open up to and everything. And even though nothing had happened in the past two years, her boyfriend started telling her, "Well, you know, you ought to do something about it."

Ellen's daughter, who was living with her father at the time, told the child welfare authorities. Ellen constantly flicked the ashes of her cigarette as she recounted how it happened:

> She went to somebody at Child Protective Services because she said she saw a program on incest, on the Phil Donahue show. And she got to thinking about it and thought everything over and thought that's what she'd better do. And they put her into temporary protective custody.

In one instance, the mother's underlying suspicions led her to disclose the incest to someone outside the family. Diane explained that in the case of her younger daughter, it was the prodding of her therapist that led her to acknowledge out loud what she suspected:

> Within twelve months I lost thirteen members of my family. I couldn't handle things so I did go to a psychiatrist and they helped me eventually face this. . . . We were discussing the marital discontent, the fact that he finally told me to leave. "Why don't you just leave and I'll keep the kids." And as I recalled, I refused. I told him "I can't leave." And the psychiatrist says, "Well, why can't you?" And I just said "I just can't leave my kids there with him." And she just kept digging until eventually I admitted—out loud— for the first time—that I could not leave because I suspected my husband was molesting my daughter.

The kinds of disclosure the mothers described suggest that whether the disclosure is private or public is more significant than if it is accidental or purposeful. There may be many mothers about whom we know little since they never came to the attention of professional helpers or social service agencies because (1) they believed they had confronted the incest and in so doing had acted protectively, (2) they may have felt too ashamed to reveal the incest event to outsiders, (3) they had little confidence in community services and how professionals would respond, or (4) they were intimidated by the father to suppress the incest and keep it a secret. The entrance into the family of an outside professional with legal authority is always a crisis-ridden event, but it may be the best insurance that the incest will not continue and that the family receives help. The daughter of one of the mothers interviewed for this study said, "Nothing could have been worse than having it continue as it did."

The Mothers' Previous Knowledge

> I had no idea anything was going on. They
> say there's signs and things you can see.
> Well, I had no idea, none whatsoever.
> (Cathy)

While there is considerable disagreement about how much a mother can know of the incest while it occurs, I was not concerned with examining the mothers' psychological defense systems of denial, nor did I attempt to verify the answser to the question, "Did she or didn't she know?" I was more interested in the mothers' explanations about how they knew, if they did, and the reasons they gave for not knowing, if they said they did not.

SUSPECTED

Two of the mothers in this book suspected the incest. Diane and Ellen were not surprised when they learned about the incest because for them it was a familiar family event. They had both been sexually abused themselves by a male family member, and Diane's oldest daughter had previously been sexually abused by her father. Diane also pondered her husband's attitudes about sex between adults and children, which added to her suspicions that her husband might be sexually abusing her younger daughter:

> I don't even know when I became suspicious of it. But I do know that between the time that he molested by older daughter and the time he molested the younger one, he had made remarks at different times that he thought maybe society was wrong. That these children should be educated like some tribes take the youngsters and do this and that.

Ellen told me she had strongly suspected her husband was molesting her daughter but was still surprised when she learned her suspicions were valid. Her shock was evident as she remembered her feelings, not so much about the sexual abuse itself, but about the age of her daughter when it began:

> When I found out [from the authorities] my ex had been molesting my daughter all these years, it blew my mind. My mind was like fireworks going off. At first I was stunned. But yet, I knew. I had my suspicions, like after she went to live with her father. But I was shocked because I hadn't suspected it at the age of three.

When suspicious, what did the mother do with her suspicions? If she failed to act, was she condoning the incest? Diane tried to justify her inability to confront either her daughter or her husband about just a hunch, with no tangible evidence:

> I felt I would lose my daughter if I asked her, that she would think I was accusing her. And I didn't want to do that. I got to the point where I thought it was going on, but I didn't know how to approach it with her or him. Because I am sure he would have denied it, and I think she would have became very indignant that I could have thought or even asked about it. I think she would have become very upset. . . . The thing is, you don't talk about this. You don't sit down at the kitchen table and say, "Well, your Dad molested your older sister when she was nine. Is he molesting you?"

While unable to approach her younger daughter directly, Diane did ask her older daughter to approach her sister:

> I had my older daughter—she's very close to my younger daughter—to ask her about it. . . . And my older daughter asked her about it, telling her, you know—"it happened to me, you should talk to Mom"—this kind of thing. But she still wouldn't say anything, not even to her sister.

Ellen explained that she had reported her earlier suspicions to the authorities at the time her daughter chose to live with her father, but during the investigation her daughter would not confirm Ellen's suspicions nor would she talk to the authorities.

> So the CPS came and interviewed the kid, but she wouldn't say anything. And it just made me look like I was making this all up. So I just dropped it. I tried to talk to my daughter about it. She wouldn't open up. And then she and my ex moved down south.

DID NOT KNOW

It is difficult for persons outside the incest-family to believe a mother really does not know that her child is being sexually abused by her husband. How can we possibly understand what appears to be the most destructive kind of denial from the perspective of the mother?

Four of the mothers in this study claimed they really did not know about the incest while it was going on. Cathy thoughtfully looked back and asserted she could not see any of the telltale signs. According to her recollections, the behavioral indicators just were not present.

> I've tried. I thought—everybody says there's telltale signs that you can tell from this or that. Well, I think he leaned over backward not to let there be any signs. And her school work didn't fall off. She didn't avoid him. When she'd go to bed at night, she'd come over and kiss me good night and then she'd go over and sit on her father's lap and hug and kiss him good night. She didn't act afraid of him or afraid to be around him.

Fay admitted she could remember some of the signs and indicators that should have alerted her to the incest if she had only interpreted them correctly:

> When I think back now, she had become very reserved, very nervous. Her grades went down the tubes. She's had four detention slips, and she never, never had detention. And she's been very uptight and acting very immature. She's doing very babyish things.

Bonnie, like Fay, acknowledged this kind of retrospective knowledge. Somewhere in her consciousness she knew something was wrong in the way her daughter behaved toward her husband:

> This is where my head knows it happened. I used to say she treated him like a wife. She was so independent and mature—she could have had her own apartment at the age of four.

As Bonnie continued, she recalled that while some signs were present, others, which might have more obviously pointed to what was going on, were missing. And her own interpretation of certain behaviors did not lead her to conclude that incest was the cause:

> I can see the psychological signs, the inappropriate behavior between her and my husband, but I still—I truly have searched to the very depths. I have no recollection of him slipping into her bedroom—but there were nightmares. There were no physical, vaginal or anal, irritations. I thought the night terrors were a spin-off of the convulsions she had as a child. There was no decline in her school work. There were none of the clues I had read about.

The mother's absence is a common explanation, as well as an indictment of her for not knowing about the incest. Fay said she did not know because she was not there when it happened. She was at work:

> It was done so sneakily. I'd go off to work, and when I came home she'd be in bed sleeping. Everything was kept so under wraps.

Bonnie claimed her sleeping pattern was the reason she did not know:

> I'm a hyperactive adult, and when I'm awake, I race. So I'm to bed around eight or nine p.m. I really burn out early. She said it happened after I went to bed. She had her own bedroom and I always went to bed by myself. It was not like he and I went to bed together and then there was a creaking noise I would have been aware of.

Ann spoke of her ignorance of the possibility of such a thing as incest as a reason for not being aware of or seeing the clues to knowing.

> I've searched and searched. How innocent I was. I just never dreamed a man would do something like this.

Ann's disbelief that incest could happen in her family is not unlike society's historical denial that the sexual abuse of children can and does happen. Today, with the increased knowledge we have about the behavioral indicators and the family dynamics of incest, even some professionals are still reluctant to face their suspicions, without any tangible evidence, that incest may be occurring in a family, particularly when the family appears to be functional in other ways.

For the most part, the families in this book were functional in the more expected ways: most of the fathers were good wage earners and supported their families economically; the mothers took care of and did not neglect their children. At the same time, all the mothers were very forthright about their difficult and problematic marriages, but they simply did not see that as a reason to suspect incest. Ellen indignantly asserted:

Well, even if you hated your husband, I'm sure you wouldn't suspect him of molesting your child. And that's how I felt.

Bonnie just could not see the dysfunction in her family as an indicator of incest. She defended her perspective:

Look, I know I had a fucked-up family. A lot of families are fucked up. You see it all the time, and I'm sure the men are not molesting their kids in all those families.

And if the mother experienced the marital relationship positively, as Cathy did, there was even less reason to suspect sexual abuse. Cathy described her situation:

It wasn't like I was denying him sex or like I was making him real unhappy. He was happy with me. I was doing what I was supposed to be doing, and I wasn't failing in any way. Our sex life was great. He had no reason to turn to my daughter.

The mothers' previous knowledge of the incest before disclosure is not as clear as we might like it to be. It is not a simple matter of whether the mother knew or did not know, consciously or unconsciously. Society expects mothers to be all knowing about what goes on in the family and the home. And as the mothers in this book have suggested, there are complex explanations for why any mother may not recognize, see, acknowledge, interpret, understand, or know a multitude of things that happen to her children.

I have chosen not to examine or explain any aspects of the mothers' defensive denial or to judge whether they knew or did not know about the incest while it was going on. Yet, I cannot ignore that denial in its different forms is a powerful force in any family whenever there are problems. I am inclined to believe that any denial underlying the explanations the mothers gave for why they did not know about the incest may have been in the service of the best choice any one of the mothers could make at that time. More critical is the fact that when the secret was revealed, all the mothers rose above whatever denial may have been operating before disclosure and believed that the incest had occurred.

The Mothers' Initial Responses to Disclosure

> I didn't deny it. I just didn't accept it.
> (Bonnie)

When informed of the incest, some mothers say they do not believe that it really happened.[2] And I am sure there are many who do not. But there is an explanation for what appears to be the initial disbelief of some mothers. Margaret Myer noted in her study of mothers that their initial disbelief and denial about the incest event after disclosure was a natural, defensive reaction to a sudden shock, not unlike the denial in the first stage of the grieving process over loss or death.[3] Bonnie made a similar analogy as she talked about her initial response to learning about the incest:

> The death-and-dying counselors talk about the five stages of denial, anger, everything else. You might find there's a pattern in how mothers [in study] handle it and zero in on it where they're at now. Is it still denial? I don't know. I'd like to see where I am in five years.

The mothers in this book displayed two initial response patterns: a disbelief/belief pattern, which was more cognitive, and a denial/acceptance pattern, which was more emotional. The two patterns, as well as the two dimensions of each pattern, were not dichotomous or discreet but rather flowed from one to the other. Suzanne Sgroi warns that a mother's initial reactions might wane or change, but she offers little to suggest or explain the mother's initial and possible contradictory feelings when she learned about the incest.[4] All the mothers who spoke with me believed cognitively that the incest had really happened, regardless of how they learned about it. At the same time, some emotionally denied the incest and could not accept it. For example, Cathy and Fay emotionally denied the reality of the incest, but they still knew and believed it had happened.

Cathy described what a profound shock the disclosure of the incest had been for her:

> At first you deny it's true. When the police came to the door and read the charges to my husband, I thought, "This can't be happening. This is a nightmare. I don't know why he doesn't get up and tell them this isn't so."

Fay, still within 24 hours of learning about the incest, was in a kind of shock. She was able to verbalize how unreal it was to her:

> It's been like a nightmare, I guess. It's been very—it seems like everything I do doesn't really feel like it's really happening.

Ellen and Diane, who had been sexually abused as children and had suspected what was going on, had less difficulty with initial denial and were more able to accept what had happened to their daughters. Ann was at the other extreme in knowing or acknowledging to herself that such a thing as incest was possible. Incest was not even a word in her vocabulary, yet she, too, like Ellen and Diane, fully believed and emotionally accepted, at two different times in her life, that her daughters and a granddaughter had been sexually abused by her husband, even while she was emotionally denying inside that such a thing was possible.

For the mothers in this book, emotional denial, when it occurred, accompanied cognitive belief. In time the denial grew into acceptance on an emotional level. Bonnie intellectually believed that the incest had occurred, but she could not emotionally accept it. She confided that she was still denying that the incest really happened a year and a half after her daughter told her about it:

> I've still emotionally denied that it happened. Right now it's my mental thing that I haven't accepted it. I haven't hit the deep depths of accepting it did happen and what really happened to my daughter. I'm still on the superficial level.

A year later I had a follow-up interview with Bonnie. A younger cousin had recently revealed that she had also been molested by Bonnie's husband when she was 14, at the same time he was molesting his stepdaughter. Bonnie was relieved, and she admitted this new information made it easier for her to move from emotional denial to emotional acceptance:

> This was the final proof. If I ever had any doubts, this was the lid on my denial. It did not shatter me. My cushion of denial just shrank. I really wanted to believe my daughter totally, and I felt guilty over not believing her. Maybe it was because there were certain things I should have done. I should have been angry [about the incest] more. I should have pressured her [her daughter] more to report it [for prosecution]. If my cousin reported it, it might not have happened to my daughter.

Margaret Myer noted in her study of incest-family mothers:

> For some women the initial reaction of denial is very short lived, while for others it can be a period of days or even longer, and some will never accept that it has happened.[5]

The reactions of the mothers I interviewed suggest that initial responses should not be interpreted as representing permanent feelings, but ought rather to be understood as normative responses in a sequence of both cognitive and emotional reactions. These responses need the support of professionals and sometimes the leverage of legal systems in the community, however difficult and painful, which can legitimize and reinforce a mother's own feelings.

Beneath what may appear to be the mothers' disbelief or denial is the reality of what they will have to do, and this means making hard choices. As already noted, mothers may be less able to initiate and follow through with protective action if they have to confront their husbands alone. Likewise, mothers may find it more difficult to move from disbelief and denial toward belief and acceptance and subsequent action without the support and assistance of professional outsiders.

When the incest secret was uncovered and revealed, all of the mothers in this book believed the incest had occurred, even while they expressed shock and disbelief, or had some difficulty fully accepting it emotionally. But once the secret was out, it raised certain questions for the mothers. Why hadn't their daughters told them about the incest while it was going on? Of all people, why did they keep the secret from their mothers? We now turn to some of the issues involved in "keeping the secret."

FOUR

Keeping the Secret

Why didn't you tell me?
(Bonnie)

Why don't daughters tell their mothers when they are being sexually abused by their fathers? Why do they keep the incest a secret? Some reasons that have been put forth are a daughter's perception of her mother's helplessness and fragility and her inability to "take care of herself, much less protect the daughter"; coercion or rewards from the father, and the disturbed mother-daughter relationship.[1]

The mothers who spoke with me gave similar reasons for why they thought their daughters did not tell them about the incest while it was going on. But as they told me their stories, it soon became clear that these reasons are better understood within the context of the husband-wife, the father-daughter, and the mother-daughter relationships.

The Husband-Wife Relationship: Power Relations

Much of the literature stresses the mothers' helplessness as a reason why daughters do not tell their mothers or enlist their aid to stop the incest.[2] Kirson Weinberg summarizes the general opinion held by many:

> The mother is the crucial controlling agent in the incest affair; and her reactions largely determine whether the affair is kept secret by the father and the daughter, or becomes known to the other family members; whether the father can continue to seduce or force several daughters into the incest relationship. The forceful, protective mothers are a minority among the incest cases, because the majority of mothers are so passive and intimidated by the father.[3]

But not all the mothers in this book pointed to their own helplessness as a possible reason for their daughters not telling them about the incest, nor did they all feel intimidated by their husbands. The degree to which they felt powerless, however, was related to how they defined their relationships with their husbands.

Nicholas Groth describes two prominent patterns of husband-wife role relationships in incest-families.[4] The first is the aggressive/dominant husband, who occupies a dominant position in the family and chooses and marries a child-wife. He maintains his power by keeping his wife and children economically dependent on him and socially isolated from relationships outside the family. "Sexual access to the daughter is experienced as part of his narcissistic entitlement and right as head of the family."[5] The second pattern is the passive/dependent husband, who is more of a dependent, needy child and marries a wife-mother. When the wife tires of fulfilling his excessive emotional needs and withdraws, the husband turns to his daughter, who is expected to take care of him.

But the husband-wife role relationship patterns described above were not as clearly distinguishable for the mothers with whom I spoke. Cathy disagreed with the way her husband defined their relationship, but she didn't take him too seriously, either:

> He used to tell me that I was a little girl when he married me and that he raised me to be the way he wanted me. I just laughed at him and thought, "Well, if that's the way he wants to think. . . ." But I didn't feel like his mother either. No, I didn't feel like his mother or his child.

While Fay saw herself in both the child and mother roles at different times, she described her husband as primarily a "father figure":

> I was a little bit of both a parent and a child to him. He knew how to do everything. He was just very intelligent and a jack-of-all-trades—super talented. He's eighteen years older than I am and in a way he's a father figure. But then a lot of times when he's had problems, I had to be the stronger figure. I had to be the one to put my foot down and show him the way. But, I guess mostly he's been a father figure to me.

Bonnie had no trouble seeing herself as a child in her marriage, but she also recounted how she took on many of the financial responsibilities in the marriage:

> Oh, I definitely see myself as a child-wife, but there was a mother side to the relationship, too. He wanted to play the masculine thing. "I'll take care of you." But he didn't. He never carried a financial crisis on his back and that's one of the reasons I went back to work full time. I took care of him in that way. I was expected to take care of the problems of living, the money, the bills.

The husband-wife role relationship patterns of the mothers above were blurred and not as clear cut as Groth's typology. Much more clear were the ways the mothers defined and perceived their husbands as more powerful than themselves, particularly if we look at abuse as a form of power. And all the mothers encountered some form of physical or psychological abuse, but they did not all respond in the same ways.[6]

PHYSICAL ABUSE

Five of the mothers were physically abused at one time or another. Bonnie described the one beating she suffered from her husband, which her five-year-old daughter witnessed, when he did not like the way she behaved at a party:

> I walked in the door. He started punching and hitting me and slammed me against the TV set and I saw stars just like in the cartoons. I had a coat on, and it was torn. The whole shoulder seam was ripped. I remember screaming for my daughter to call the police. I probably tried to defend myself, but he was one hundred eighty pounds, six foot two inches tall. I was about ninety-five pounds and under five feet. I ended up with a concussion. I was never beaten up again, but I was physically afraid of him after that. I still am.

Bonnie said she was in constant fear of her husband while they were married and offered her daughter's perception of her helplessness as a possible reason for not telling:

> Why didn't she come to me and say, "Daddy is doing this. Make him stop"? I think it was because she saw me as a very weak person. She saw my fear of him. She would never have thought I had the power to make him stop. I had no power in that house. . . . I just don't think she thought I could do anything. . . . Maybe she feared if she told me and I didn't do anything—God! It would have probably devastated her.

Within the home Bonnie looked like one kind of a woman—passive, helpless, and fearful. She was realistically afraid of what her husband might do, but that did not mean she was necessarily a passive person. Bonnie explained that outside the house she was assertive, competent, and unafraid.

> Right about then, when I was becoming successful in business, I became very concerned that my daughter saw me in my home-life as a very down-trodden individual. I mean, I was a real peon. When my husband said "Jump," I said, "How high?" But I wanted to pull her aside and say, "You think I'm downtrodden, but let me tell you about work."

Fay, too, was afraid of her husband and talked about what he was capable of when he had been drinking:

> I was afraid of him when he got in his tempers. He would destroy the whole house. I mean, he wouldn't think anything about taking the table and throwing it through the window. He's hit me. I wouldn't say physically abused me, beat me up, but from anger he's hit me. It was always when he was drunk. It only happened two times. Considering his personality I suppose it could have been a lot worse. He would just pick out something to be mad at, something small, and just make it into something real big, and then he would just blow up. He would think nothing of destroying the house, putting holes in the wall.

For Ellen the physical abuse was part of a violent family life-style. She came from a family where she witnessed continual, severe, physical battles between her mother and father that often led to police intervention. She married a man who beat her, blamed her for whatever went wrong, and threatened her. She described an incident early in their marriage:

> When my daughter was six months old, I had asked him to take me to the laundromat because I didn't have a washing machine, and he got mad. I was down to using towels for diapers. So right in front of his little teenage buddy he beat the holy hell out of me, and I mean he kicked me in the back and the stomach and punched me in the face. I called the police on him. I had him arrested. But later I dropped the charges. I talked his way out of it, if that makes any sense. I was sticking up for him, saying it was all my fault. You see, all through my marriage I knew I was sick, because I blamed myself for all of this, but today I know it's not all my fault.

While Bonnie and Fay were cautious and wary of their husbands to prevent further abuse, and Ellen almost accepted marital violence as a way of life, Cathy and Diane did not condone that kind of behavior and were more openly assertive in the ways they responded to their husbands' physical abuse. Cathy told me she was not used to, nor did she tolerate, her husband's abuse:

> He used to slap me around and stuff when the girls were little. Then I got to the point where I thought, "I'm not going to take this off of him," and I fought back. If he started to hit me, I'd pick up anything I could get my hands on and hit him back. See, he's six feet tall, and I'm about five feet two inches. And he weighs about two hundred pounds, so he's real big. At first I wouldn't do anything if he'd hit me or anything. Then I thought, "Hey, I'm not his punching bag, and I'm not going to stand there and just let him hit me." I didn't want him to think that he could just do whatever he wanted to me, and that I was going to stand there and take it, because he always acted like he was big and I was little, so I had to do what he said. Well, I didn't feel that way.

Diane put up with her husband's physical attacks for a while, but she soon found a way to combat them. As if confiding a secret weapon to me she recounted the last abusive incident:

> I was all black and blue, and I refused to wear a long-sleeved shirt. And if anybody said to me, "How did you get all black and blue?" I'd tell them, "My husband beat me." And they laughed. They thought I was making a big joke. But my husband knew. He sat there, and he knew. He understood and he never tried it again.

PSYCHOLOGICAL ABUSE

Another way a husband manifested his power over his wife was through psychological abuse, which Mildred Pagelow defines as "an experience in denigration of self that results in diminished self-esteem . . .

shame and feelings of worthlessness."[7] Five of the mothers told of experiencing some form of psychological abuse. Ellen described the way her husband treated her as threatening and demeaning.

> Every time we'd get into an argument he'd say he was taking his daughter and leaving. . . . I always felt guilty because if anything happened bad in the marriage, it was my fault. It was always my fault when he left. . . . When you were married to [her husband] you don't feel like—how can I put it? You just felt like an object—like a chair, really. Something that he used and phffft, he didn't want anymore.

For Ann the psychological abuse was quite different. Ann had been admitted to a psychiatric facility—an admission precipitated by her discovery of her husband's sexual abuse of their oldest daughter and the stress of keeping the secret after her husband assured her that it was not serious and that she was overreacting. The psychological abuse Ann remembered was pervasive and insidious:

> I didn't have very positive feelings about being signed out of the hospital into his care. There was a lot of fear about that. I really felt he held—depending on which way I jumped or what I did—he had the power or the control over what happened to me.

Ann continued, telling me how her husband's control over her instilled deep fears in her about herself. As she talked, I thought of the ways a woman can be "gaslighted" by a man who can make her believe things about herself that are not true:

> I was afraid emotionally or psychologically that the things he could say to me could make me feel better or worse. . . . I had a sense from some of the things he said that there were grounds for me to feel that way, truly. I very much had the feeling that he was the control. He had the power to work me into a state of putting me back into the hospital. My main concern was to stay on an even keel and carry on my life as I believed in it.

During the time I met with Ann she sent for her hospital records. The admission notes stated:

> Admitted . . . with a history of depression. Thought content confused, speech tangential and extremely circumstantial, bothered by recurrent obsessions involving incest.

Now, 20 years after that psychiatric admission for what was probably a transient, reactive depression, Ann still feared her husband. With great difficulty she confronted him on the phone within a month after leaving him when she learned that he had gone on to sexually abuse both their daughters and, within that past year, a granddaughter.

Bonnie described the psychological abuse she experienced from her husband in terms of the worthlessness she felt:

He made me feel worthless. He was the most demeaning person. He stripped you of all your self-worth. You didn't just burn a dinner; you were no good at doing anything. . . . I was constantly being yelled at, screamed at, sworn at. He was base. The atmosphere was vile.

Fay related more the shame she felt and the emotional costs of her husband's psychological abuse, feeling this was worse than any physical abuse she suffered:

I don't want to be criticized. I don't want to be walked on. I don't want to be pushed around. I've gone through too many years of violence. In this marriage I had more emotional abuse, and that sometimes is worse than physical abuse. I've been emotionally abused because I lived with a sick person for four years. I had to swallow my pride and ask people for money because my husband gambled it away or drank it away. I had to ask people to buy my children clothes and shoes because of him. I felt like I had been walked on and kicked around and just beat up emotionally, and I'm just emotionally drained right now. Sometimes emotional abuse is worse than physical abuse.

In general, the mothers who suffered psychological abuse, either by itself or in addition to physical abuse, responded with caution and wariness to their husbands' intimidation of them. Bonnie, for example, spoke of how she was afraid to fight back openly:

I was the little, docile, Chinese wife three steps behind the man. I never tested him. I would just respond if he told me to do something. I was a downtrodden peon. I paid lip service. I never talked back and I never fought back.

Ann, probably the most helpless-looking of all the mothers, admitted her fear to do or say anything that might set her husband off:

In other words, to criticize him, or to talk about a situation about everyday living—I backed off from doing that because I couldn't shed the fear of his control.

Diane had been brought up to accept her husband's authority; the father was the head of the household, the "governing force, with the mother having no say in anything." But Diane said she was beginning to think differently about talking back:

Thinking back, I think the woman should be more outspoken, even if it does mean a fight. Although you know you don't want to argue in front of the children, there comes a point when you have to decide between being walked on or arguing in front of your children, if that's what it takes.

Diane described how she eventually stood up for herself:

> I did talk back to him, finally. I refused to let him rule me. There are times
> when I think he still tries to manipulate me as he has done for years. For
> instance, I'm heavy. I know I'm heavy, but as far back as I can remember,
> he constantly put me down. He still tries it. But now I don't let him. Before
> I let him. I let him beat me down. He really made me feel stupid, although
> I know I'm not. I did then, because he told me I was stupid. But not anymore.

All the mothers in this book described their husbands as men who
asserted themselves as authoritarian heads of the household, and themselves as wives who were subject to that authority. But this did not mean
they perceived themselves as fragile and powerless within all areas of
their lives or that they were always passive or helpless in their responses
to the different kinds of abuse they suffered. Ann and Bonnie saw their
own powerlessness and helplessness vis-à-vis their husbands as a possible
reason for their daughters not telling them about the incest event. The
other mothers found reasons within other family relationships.

The Father-Daughter Relationship: Coercion, Rewards, Role Confusion

There is little information about the father-daughter relationship apart
from or beyond the incest event itself. Daughters are said to split their
images of their fathers. They "describe their fathers as perfect patriarchs"
but also "express some warm feelings" toward them.[8] "They were daddy's
special girls"[9] and had a special alliance, favored treatment, and fond
memories of their relationships with their fathers.[10]

The mothers did not view the father-daughter relationship as clearly
or with as much feeling as they did their own relationships with their
husbands. But from their viewpoint, there were three features, however
weak, related to their daughters' reluctance to tell them about the incest
event. These features were coercion, rewards, and role confusion.

COERCION

Threats are one way to reinforce secrecy. Threats can be in the form
of anger, separation, or harm to the child or someone else or can be more
subtle or implied, stemming from family violence.[11]

The mothers with whom I spoke did not provide any clear, specific
information about their husbands threatening to do anything to their
daughters if they did not go along with or if they told anyone about the
incest. They spoke more from inference and a sense of what might have
happened.

Ann had been hospitalized for what was then described as a nervous
breakdown. Ann told me how her husband used her tenuous nervous

condition and absence from the home to let his daughters know what the consequences of telling would be:

> As far as I know, from what they've told me, I think they were threatened with telling—that something would happen to their mother. That's the loudest and clearest that comes out.

Fay spoke of her daughter's fear of her stepfather based on his out-of-control behavior, a good illustration of an implied threat:

> He never threatened her, like, "I'll beat you" or anything like that. I don't even know if she knew what she was afraid of. She was afraid of the unknowing. "Dad's going to get mad at me, and when he gets mad, watch out." She was afraid of him in a lot of ways because he did have such a violent temper. He was so physical—knocking tables over, punching holes in the wall. That would scare her. She was afraid he was going to be angry with her.

Cathy focused on her husband's drinking and how she saw that affecting his relationship with his daughters:

> When he would get mad, more because of his drinking than anything, he would get real mad. When they'd do something he didn't like, he'd overreact and over-punish them. He'd get mad if they didn't come right home from school. When he was working, he never drank during the day, but when he was laid off he'd drink all day long. He was really unpredictable. Sometimes he'd be fine—he'd be real good. Other times, he would just gripe about anything he could find to gripe about. They weren't really afraid of him, of him hitting them or anything like that. He didn't get violent. He would just pick on them. And he was always real overreactive to everything they did.

Here again is another example of an implied threat, based on Cathy's projection of her husband's potential behavior when he drank. Cathy continued, still relating her husband's unpredictable behavior to his drinking:

> I think it's only been the past five years or so that he's been like this—when he really started drinking heavier. At first he would just blow up a little bit, and it would be over real quick. It dropped almost as soon as it began. And then it would go on longer and get real radical. Real fine one minute and the next—it would be little things that he would really blow up about. Like if the girls wouldn't do the dishes right away. This is a normal thing. But he'd start screaming and yelling at them, and he'd go on and on, and they'd try to explain, and then it was even worse. "Don't talk back to me. I'm your father." And if they were real insistent on it, he might slap them, just once.

Except for Ann, coercion was not presented by the mothers as a strong reason for keeping the incest secret. Nor were rewards.

REWARDS

Ellen and Fay were the only mothers who mentioned rewards from the father as a possible reason for their daughters not telling them about the incest. Ellen admitted her confusion about the relationship between her daughter and husband, which was still evident as she talked:

> I never could figure out why this kid wanted to go live with her father except that he spoiled her rotten. . . . She's a very manipulating young woman. I know she used sex to get anything she wanted. . . . In fact, I asked her why she didn't tell me when she had the chance, and she didn't have any answer. . . . I told her, "I think you were using it to get what you wanted." And she said, "You're right."

There was another kind of a reward, a reward for a child who, for the first time, had a father. Fay had married her husband when her daughter was seven years old. She explained what this relationship must have meant to her daughter:

> He's the only father she ever knew. She's never known anybody really as a father before I married him. . . . But he never showed her a lot of love and care. He would say, "Yes, I love you," or "Yes, I'm concerned about you." But he wouldn't in a real fatherly way show it. . . . Oh, at times he would hug her and say, "I love you." He was able to show compassion and tell her, "Everything's okay, you can talk to me." For instance, the school called to say she had detention. I was very upset and very angry with her. But he said, "Let me go and pick her up and talk to her." He was understanding, where on the other hand, I was the angry one.

Here it was the stepfather who was the reward and who in some way compensated for Fay, who described herself as an angry, strict parent, even more strict than her husband: "I was the quicker one to slap her." She taught her daughter to obey her stepfather, and in so doing she feared she may have put her daughter in a double bind. Fay's daughter obeyed her stepfather when he told her not to tell anyone about the incest event, because she was afraid both of disobeying her mother and him and of losing him, her new father.

Thus far, the mothers did not provide enough evidence to attribute coercion or rewards as strong enough reasons for keeping the secret—at least not from their perspectives. What I am going to look at now is what they said about the relationships between their husbands and daughters, reconstructing those relationships in terms of an idea presented by Nicholas Groth, which I call "role confusion."

ROLE CONFUSION

Nicholas Groth explains that incest offenders experience the child sexual partner as a pseudo adult,[12] and in so doing, the incest-father abandons his parental role. In some instances the mother might also perceive her daughter as more of an adult than a child in relationship to her father. Bonnie described the relationship between her daughter and husband in just this way:

> I used to say she treated him like a wife. He was a pathological liar, and she would pin him on his lies, unlike a child to her father. . . . Once on a trip she did something that really upset him. She ignored him, and he got drunk and was going to go home alone because she had ignored him, like his girlfriend had upset him.

Ellen talked about how others described the inappropriate "adult" closeness between her daughter and husband:

> My ex and I split up when she was ten, and she chose to go live with her father. . . . People would tell me, "There's something wrong. If you could see the way your husband and daughter are with each other." Friends said they looked like lovers walking up the street holding hands. And he would put his arm around her like she was his girlfriend. My sister told me when they'd visit her that my daughter would sit in his lap and blow kisses in his ear. . . . This is a grown man and his daughter, and she loves him like a husband.

In addition, Ellen felt her husband and daughter shared a special bond, a special togetherness from which she was excluded. There was still pain in her voice as she spoke:

> I always felt as if I was on the outside with them. From the moment she was born, they had a special bond. He was as proud as a peacock when she was born. He was real good with her. He helped bathe and feed her. He rocked her and changed her diapers and was an expert on her diet. Because he didn't like a certain food, she didn't like it. But I thought, "This is his first born, so maybe that's why he spent so much time with her". . . . He was a totally doting father on that child. He spoiled her rotten.

In contrast to Bonnie and Ellen, who saw their daughters behaving more as adults than as children in relationship to their fathers, Cathy described more of a family of children growing up together, and a closeness between her daughter and husband that did not exclude her:

> And we've always been really involved with the girls as far as anything they were involved in—like going to band practice. Most other parents would just go to the band competition, but we'd go to every practice. We would take them to the Boys' Club and stay while they did their gymnastics. Him and I and two other parents went and hid the eggs in the park so that the kids could have an Easter egg hunt. They did a lot of things through the Boys' Club—field trips and camp—and instead of them going on the buses, we took them and went and got them. . . . We've always gone camping together, and because he was off work a lot in the winter, we'd sit around and play games

with the kids instead of watching TV. They loved it when the electric would go out, because then we would have the kerosene lamps lit, and we'd sit around playing monopoly or cards. So, we've always been—our kids were number one. We didn't leave them and go off. When he was off work, it was always everything together.

In Cathy's family the father-daughter bond was within the boundary that enclosed and included all family members. Togetherness was a family theme pervading many arenas of family life and resembled what Salvador Minuchin has described as "family enmeshment," which results from a blurring or diffusion of boundaries between family subsystems.[13] Cathy went on to describe the way her husband played with their daughters:

> He played a lot of physical things outside with the girls. He would play anything with them outdoors. But he used to play with them in the house, too. He would hold their dolls, and I have a lot of pictures of him playing with their dolls, where they would bring them to him and say, "Will you hold my baby? Will you give it the bottle while I go and do this or that?" And he would. He'd play their doll games with them.

Cathy also talked about another dimension of her husband's peer relationship with his daughters, an open sexuality fully accepted by her:

> He used to bathe with the girls when they were little until they were preschool age, and then he would take them in and play with them in the bathtub, play with their ducks, bubble baths, and all that. I liked doing that, too. Before they were school-age, once they started really asking questions and realizing the difference between men and women, then he would always wear something, even if it was only a towel wrapped around him. I can remember one time one of the girls ran up behind him and picked up the towel and went "woo-wee," and peeked under the towel. So they knew the difference. They knew that was something they weren't supposed to do, that it was kind of a little joke.

There seemed to be an open sexual attitude that what was appropriate behavior for adults was okay for children, too. Cathy unabashedly told me about their *Playboy* magazines.

> He always had *Playboy* magazines around the house, and the girls knew they were allowed to look at them. They were never forbidden to look at them if they wanted to. It was just open in that way.

As she talked, Cathy also conveyed an openness about sexual information, which she attributed to their youth as parents:

> We were both very open with the girls about sex. Mostly when the girls and I would have conversations about sex, he'd be around and it didn't matter to

them if he was around or not. Mostly it was because he and I were so young when we got married. We kind of grew up at the same time that we were raising the girls, and him and I were real open.

Cathy remembered fondly a photograph incident at the beach:

> I can remember when they were little [under seven] . . . we had gone to the beach, and I'd give them all a shower to get all the sand off, and he'd come down with the camera because they all had little, white buns, and they all turned with their buns to the camera to model for him how their white buns showed up. When they first came out with the underwear that had the panties and bras that matched for little girls, and they all got a pair of those and they all modeled for him, and he was going to take a picture of them, and they all stood there with their hands on their hips and in like a sexy pose.

Cathy's description of the close relationship between her husband and daughters was unique among the mothers in this book, as was the open sexuality that smudged appropriate boundaries between the generations.

The four mothers in this study who spoke about the father-daughter relationship constructed it in different ways. Coercion and rewards from the father may have gone hand in hand. And an open sexual family life-style may have been evident, as in Cathy's case. But coercion and rewards were not among the reasons the mothers gave for their daughters keeping the secret secret from them.

The mothers went on to make further connections between their own relationships with their daughters and the secret their daughters kept.

The Mother-Daughter Relationship: "Essential and Distorted"[14]

The literature has been very critical of the mother-daughter relationship in incest families and has pointed particularly to role reversal as a contributing factor to the incest event.[15] Judith Herman writes, "At best daughters viewed their mothers ambivalently," and at worst their relationships were "marked by active hostility."[16] Daughters are reported to have felt alienated from their mothers, whose roles they felt obligated to fulfill, and it was "in the special alliance with their fathers that they felt loved and cared for."[17] Yet, this assumption that all mothers and daughters are estranged and that role reversal is a common dynamic in the mother-daughter relationship is not empirically founded. Karin Meiselman and Barbara Brooks found no evidence in their studies that the pattern of role reversal was prevalent in incest-families.[18] Likewise, none of the mothers in this book believed that their daughters took over their roles in the family, and only Ellen characterized her relationship with her daughter as hostile, alienated, and conflicted.

While the incest literature is filled with daughters' descriptions of their mothers, there is little written about the mothers' perceptions of their daughters. If we listen to what the mothers in this book had to say, what might we find besides hostility, alienation, and conflict between mothers and daughters to characterize the mother-daughter relationship? And what could we learn about the possible connections between these relationships and the daughters' reluctance to tell their mothers about the incest? Two mother-daughter relationship patterns emerged as I listened to the mothers talk about their daughters: peer relationships and parent-child relationships.

PEER RELATIONSHIP PATTERNS

Bonnie's and Ellen's descriptions of what I have termed "mother-daughter peer relationships" fell into two patterns: pals and rivals. Bonnie and her daughter were "pals, tested pals." They shared sexual jokes together and her daughter advised her on how to wear makeup and how to dress. At the time I spoke with Bonnie, she told me how very involved and invested she was in her children's activities, defining this as one of the ways to be a good mother. She participated in her daughter's teenage parties as one of the gang, answering questions about sex, birth control, and how not to let the boys use you. Bonnie proudly asserted that she was a "different" kind of mother.

> I'm different from all their parents. I really want to be the friend. I don't want to be the friend they walk on, but I want to be the friend that doesn't act like I don't burp and fart and have problems.

Bonnie spoke freely about her daughter without any prompting from me. She was very proud of her, but saw her as different from herself, almost as her alter ego; and her feelings reflected more the sentiments between peers and friends than between females belonging to different generations. Both Bonnie and her daughter looked like teenagers. Bonnie was barely five feet tall and weighed 95 pounds. She had the body of a young female entering puberty, even when wearing her high fashion, dressed-for-success businesswoman's costume. But there was little sense of Bonnie's daughter parenting her or of Bonnie expecting parenting from her daughter. Bonnie looked to her daughter to meet some of her emotional needs, but again, this was within a more equal, sharing relationship than as a dependent child. She seemed to have almost erased the parent-child boundary in a desire to be closer to her daughter and to be seen and understood as human. Bonnie explained further.

> I have very few boundaries between me and the children. I want my kids to know I'm human, that I get upset, that I'm lonely, that I'm scared. . . . I'd like my daughter to see me the way I really am and for me to see her the way she really is.

Bonnie claimed a song sung by Helen Reddy, "You and Me Against the World," as their theme song, and this seemed to illustrate the emotional closeness she felt with her daughter. One of the few times Bonnie expressed deep emotional feelings during the interviews was when she quoted some of the lines from the song:

> When one of us is gone
> When one of us is left to carry on
> Remembering will have to do
> Our memories alone will carry us through.

Bonnie felt very close to her daughter, and this provided yet another reason for her daughter not to tell her about the incest, in addition to her belief that her mother would not have been able to protect her. Bonnie recounted the reason her daughter gave her for not telling:

> She said she didn't tell me because she loved me. My God! What a way to have to show a love for a mother. To have a child feel that you are so weak that you couldn't have stepped in. . . . I remember putting my arms around her and her just sobbing.

In sharp contrast, Ellen and her daughter, while peers, were more rivals than friends. Use of the term "rival" may be misleading, for Ellen expressed no direct jealousy or malice toward her daughter. However, the relationship between them was rife with estrangement and misunderstanding. Ellen said she did not blame her daughter for this state; she blamed her husband[19]:

> I believe I feel this way because my ex-husband has always put a wedge in the relationship I tried to have with my daughter.

Ellen, more than any of the other mothers, flooded the interviews with unsolicited content and feelings about her daughter. She began with the ambivalence she felt and of her very difficult pregnancy, which included severe morning sickness, bleeding, pneumonia, and physical abuse from her husband:

> I was dreading having her. I wanted her. I wanted this baby, but yet, I was getting mad at this baby because I was so sick all the time. I had a bad time giving birth to her, too. I was in labor twenty-four hours with her to top everything else off.

From the beginning Ellen felt her husband put her daughter first, focusing all his attention on the baby and ignoring her. An early separation from her daughter widened the breach. Ellen told me about it, the resentment still permeating her voice:

> The first time I felt disconnected was when my ex took her when she was

three years old to his mother's house. She was only supposed to keep her for about two weeks. They kept her for six months. I sent him down there to bring her back, and he came back without her. The next time I went with him, and I threatened him. I said, "If you go over there and don't come out with her, I'm going to call the state police." So he went and got her. This is when I first began to have that feeling. Before then, I didn't. She was just a little baby, you know. Up until three they're—she's still a baby at three.

Ellen went on to say she felt almost as if her husband was grooming her daughter to be her rival:

She was a sweet little girl and a pretty kid. She was a beautiful kid. She could have been a model. She still could be. I always wondered why we never had a decent relationship. We never had a chance. I always felt like—how can I put this? Not a woman to woman, because she wasn't a woman. She was only a kid. But I felt like I had to compete with her to get attention, which wasn't an easy thing. And how can you get mad at a kid? You can get mad at your husband, but you can't get mad at this little kid because she doesn't know. . . . Even when she was little, sometimes I resented her because that's all he wanted. I figured he was just rejecting me.

Ellen asserted that she was a good mother, despite the poor relationship she had with her daughter:

It's hard for me to really recall any relationship I had with my daughter. I mean, I bought her clothes, took care of her when she was sick, had birthday parties for her, made Christmas cookies, colored Easter eggs. I was a good mother. I really was. But I could never feel close to her.

But Ellen did describe some good moments with her daughter when her husband was gone and she was not in the position of outsider:

We had our good moments. . . . And they were always good when he was gone. But when he was around they were terrible. I never knew why, except that he favored her.

Ellen separated from her husband. This eventually entailed another separation from her daughter. Ellen recounted what happened:

When my daughter was ten my ex-husband and I separated and he asked her to go live with him. She didn't right away. I think she was kind of torn, but every night she'd come home from school, and she would mope and go right to her room. This went on for like two weeks. She would just go off to her room and stay there. She wouldn't even come out for supper. And she cried. So I finally asked her if she wanted to go live with her dad, and that's what she wanted to do. I let her. . . . And I could never figure out why this kid wanted to go live with her father except that he spoiled her rotten. But at the time I didn't want to fight it either. I was tired of fighting. I had another kid to think about, and if she was going to be happy with him—that's why

I let her go. . . . I tried to get her back when we went to get our divorce. But he threw up my first marriage and not being divorced. And my lawyer knew all about this and said, "He's got a loaded gun at your head." What are you going to do? So I let her go live with my ex.

Ellen described visits with her daughter, which were not pleasant and further widened the breach between them:

During that time I saw her when she wanted to come over. She was terrible at that point. She would go out of the house and call me a bitch. I mean yelling "You fucking bitch" right down the street. She was terrible. She went from this sweet little Brownie into a monster. . . . She's a very manipulative child. She always has been, but she was taught that from him, and if she couldn't get her own way, if I was the heavy, then she'd be mad at me.

Ellen confided her sense of failure as a mother:

I'll tell you, I felt real guilty about my relationship with her. . . . I always blamed myself for my daughter. I always felt the relationship we had wasn't good. That was my fault. I didn't try hard enough. I felt like a failure as a mother to that kid.

Ellen said she knew that somewhere there was love for her daughter—love she could not find:

When it comes to how I feel about my daughter, I just can't explain it. I just don't know what I really feel for her. I'm sure there is love somewhere in my heart for her, but I have to find it again. This has to do with losing her to the devil, my ex. In all reality, I guess it started with the incest, but I didn't know it was happening. To better explain, I feel I lost her, and I haven't found her yet. And that the incest problem is not why I feel this way.

Ellen reiterated a constant theme as she talked about her daughter and her husband. They were together and she was the outsider:

I always felt as if I was on the outside with them. From the day I brought her home from the hospital he has put her over me, and I guess maybe deep down inside I resented that. It got worse after she went to live with him and as she got older. I think it has to do with the way he kept us apart.

Today, both Ellen and her daughter admit their relationship is not good. But Ellen describes the rift more in terms of a relationship between two rival women than between a mother and her daughter:

To this day she will say we cannot get along, that we cannot live together. Let's face it, for the past seven years, pretty important years, she's been the woman of the house. And it's pretty hard for two women to live under the same roof.

Ellen believed her daughter did not tell her about the incest for telling would mean giving up the rewards she derived from her relationship with her father. And while Ellen did see her daughter usurping her position of wife, it was not because she abandoned the position but because she had been ejected from it by her husband.

Bonnie and Ellen both experienced a peer relationship with their daughters. While they did not describe what has been termed role reversal, they saw their daughters in adult roles in the father-daughter relationship and themselves more as child-wives to their husbands. In both family configurations, the mother was outside the boundary around her husband and daughter; Bonnie because she left and Ellen because her husband rejected her in favor of her daughter.

MOTHER-DAUGHTER, PARENT-CHILD RELATIONSHIP PATTERN

Cathy and Fay were quite clear about who was the mother and who was the child in the family. They saw their daughters very much as their children, and as with the "peer relationship patterns," two parent-child relationship patterns emerged: loving-close and strict-distant.

Cathy illustrated the loving-close pattern with quite a different story than Ellen's. She lovingly described her baby daughter:

> She was a perfect baby. From the moment she was born, I just felt that she was perfect in every way. She was beautiful. She looked like the Gerber baby. Everybody said so. And she was always real good natured. And I think that's one reason that I wanted another baby right away, because she just made me so happy. She was so good.

Like Ellen's husband, Cathy's husband also paid a lot of attention to his daughter, but Cathy was not threatened and did not feel rejected or left out. She delighted in the way her husband felt "there was nothing like his daughter."

Cathy recounted the pleasure she had playing with her baby and her happiness as a wife and mother:

> I just loved playing with my baby. It was kinda like being a little girl, but kinda like—you know, I was real happy. I had my baby, I had my house, I had my husband, and I was really into it. I wanted to take care of her. I used to spend so much time dressing her, and playing with her, bathing her. These are happy memories.

Joy spread across Cathy's face and filled her voice as she talked about her daughter. She described how she continued to play with her daughter even as she grew older:

> From the time she was little, I would teach her to play with toys. A lot of parents nowadays don't do that. They just give them toys and expect the kids to know how to play with them. I'd take the baby doll and hold it the way that you would hold it and talk to it, feed it with the bottle, show her

how to play with it. We used to have tea parties with nothing at all, just her and I. We'd pretend we had cups, pretend we were pouring tea, pretend we were picking up cookies and eating them. And I taught her that way—to pretend things. . . . And I read to her all the time. Her favorite story was "Pinocchio," and she'd sit there reading the story to herself. She'd imitate me like playing with her dolls, playing house. She would do it just the way I would. Like talking on the phone—she would stand the way I always stood.

Although Cathy viewed her daughter as mature and encouraged her to be independent, she did not parentify or exchange the adult, parent role with her. Cathy proudly told me how grown up and responsible her daughter was.

She was mature for her age. I depended on her to help with the baby, but I always made her feel like it wasn't a chore, that she was allowed to do it as much as I was. . . . She helped me a lot with her sisters. She started kindergarten at four because she was so mature, and she was always real good in school, always got real good grades, and the teacher would always tell me how helpful and how smart she was. . . . I never treated my daughters like babies. I never baby talked to them or babied them, or made them feel helpless. I would spend a lot of time teaching them things, helping them to do things for themselves.

In contrast to the alienation described by Ellen, Cathy talked about the closeness she felt between her daughter and herself, but not in the peer sense that Bonnie described:

I feel close to her, but I don't feel like her sister. I am her mother. She doesn't even talk back to me. The other three will, and I'll say, "Hey, I'm not your sister, I'm your mother. Don't talk to me like that". . . . She'll say her boyfriend said this, or he said that, and I'll say, "I don't care what he says. You're my baby, not his." She says she's grown up, but she's still my baby. She'll always be my baby.

Cathy claimed she felt no rivalry with her daughter, seeing a difference in the love between her husband and herself from that between her husband and their daughter:

No, I don't feel any jealousy toward my daughter. If I were jealous of her, it would be like she was meaning more to my husband than I did. And I don't feel like that. I know that he loves me. I know that he loves her, but I know that the love isn't the same.

Cathy said her daughter did not tell her about the incest because of their close relationship, a reason similar to the one Bonnie's daughter gave.

She hadn't told anybody about it. I remember saying, "Why didn't you tell me?" She said, "I didn't want to hurt you." I just couldn't believe she wouldn't tell me because I've been real open with her. And afterwards, when she told me the way she felt and everything, I did understand because her and I are so close. And she felt she was going to be hurting me by telling me this. Not because it was her that was involved or anything. She didn't want to be the one to tell me that things weren't the way I thought they were. She didn't want me to be hurt.

Like the other mothers, Cathy did not describe role reversal between herself and her daughter. Cathy appeared to be more a mother-wife than a child-wife and saw her daugher more as a peer to her husband than as an adult and herself as mother to them both. In this family configuration the family boundary did not leave anyone outside, but enclosed all members in what Cathy described as loving closeness.

In contrast to Cathy, who was a close-loving mother, Fay was a strict-distant mother and described herself as very overprotective with her daughter because of the memories of her own wild childhood. Underlying Fay's words was her fear that her daughter would make some of the same mistakes she did.

> I'm so overprotective of my daughter. I always have been. Now I'm even worse. . . . I love and protect her because I was a wild kid. I was the type of kid to go and do whatever I wanted to do. Footloose and fancy free—that's the type of kid I was.

Fay also described herself as very strict:

> Mostly I was the disciplinarian. I'm the type, if you do something I'm either going to slap you up side of the head or I'm going to sit down and tell you your punishment. But then after it's over, I love you and I'm your mother.

Later, Fay elaborated on her strict behavior, which sprang from her temper:

> I lose my temper. I would grab your hair or else slap you. I've even knocked her down, and that's awful and it's been a long time since I've done it. I've really come to grips with myself. But I used to be just awful when it comes to just not even thinking. I was the one who would physically hurt my child, and I still am the one that would slap her quicker than he ever would.

Fay thought about why her daughter might have been afraid to tell about the incest, and speculated:

> She may have felt guilty. Like probably she did something wrong because Mom always told her, "If anyone touches you, please come to me and tell me."

Fay also attributed the distance between herself and her daughter as the reason her daughter did not tell her about the incest:

If I had been a better mother, if I had let her be more open to talk to me, if I had been more of a shoulder to lean on, maybe she could have come to me. But then maybe she would still have been afraid to tell me. Mom's always too busy to sit down and listen.

Fay admitted how difficult it was and still is for her to express her love emotionally:

I would show my love by taking her out and buying her a coat or a dress, an ice cream. That's how I show my love. It's material, and that's not the right way. I would like to learn to show my love emotionally. I'm reserved. Maybe I always will be. It's my personality. She's reserved because I have always been. And that's why I have a very reserved child right now, because I've always been that way.

Fay looked to her own youth and immaturity as reasons for her lack of knowledge about mothering and talked about what a "real mom" would be like:

I think that me being a young mother had so many pressures. I didn't know what a mother was until I became a mother. Oh, so this is what a mother is. A mother is—anybody could be a mother, but I think a real mother is a friend. I think a real mom is somebody who you can turn to whenever you want. And I feel that I haven't been a real mother like I should have been. I started out being ignorant, being very immature, self-centered, about a lot of things. But I could see the things I've done wrong, and I try to take one day at a time, make it better. . . . I could have been a much better mother.

Fay was very critical of herself as a mother, reciting her mistakes as evidence. She admitted to not being very nurturing or understanding, attributing this to her need to be strong:

I've learned by my mistakes. I can't change my mistakes, but I'm trying to understand them, and I'm trying to let her know I've made mistakes, and I love her. I'm not an emotional, loving mother. I'm not one of those real lovable people. I'm very reserved with my feelings. If a child falls down and cries, I pick it up and say, "Go ahead and play." It's hard for me to get overemotional about those little tiny things that kids need. I still have problems being an understanding, compassionate, lovey-dovey mommy. I'm too busy trying to be a strong person.

Fay functioned more as a mother-wife than as a child-wife to her husband and saw herself as a mother to both her daughter and her husband. She also saw her daughter as a child to her husband. In this family the mother drew the boundary around herself and her daughter, leaving the father on the outside.

Mother-daughter relationships in incest families, as in most families, are complex. None of the mothers I interviewed identified role reversal as a pattern or key dynamic in their relationships with their daughters. They did not feel they parentified their daughters; they did not view their daughters as parents to them.

It should be kept in mind that the mothers' portrayals of family relationships may well differ from the portrayals other family members might present. However, the construction and meaning of the generational boundaries to the different incest-family members, and the way each member defined the role relationship patterns, are significant. The construction and meaning may influence the position each family member occupies within the family, as seen by other family members, and consequently their definition of the way each member performs his or her role.

The mothers who shared their perceptions with me held different ideas about why their daughters did not tell them about the incest. These ideas were not necessarily consistent with how they responded or the action they took when they learned about the incest event. We now turn to the mothers' emotional and behavioral responses following the disclosure.

FIVE

The Mothers Respond

You do what you think you have to do. You
have to keep him away from your daughter.
(Diane)

Why are some mothers able to act protectively toward their daughters
following disclosure of the incest event while others are not? As the
mothers shared their stories with me I began to realize that the contexts
of their lives were as critical to understanding their responses as their
individual characteristics. I have looked at the mothers' responses to the
disclosure of incest on two levels: emotional, in terms of what they felt,
and behavioral, in terms of what they did.

The Mothers' Emotional Responses

Earlier the mothers described their initial reactions to disclosure and
talked about whether they believed or did not believe cognitively that
the incest took place and whether they accepted or denied it emotionally.
In this section the mothers speak about their feelings when they first
learned about the incest. While the mothers reported these feelings to
me in retrospect, and it may be difficult to separate what they initially
felt from what they felt when they were talking to me, they do give us
some idea of their emotional reactions to the incest event itself, their
daughters, and their husbands.

RESPONSES TO THE INCEST EVENT

The mothers did not readily express their feelings about the incest
unless I prompted them with a question. I sensed that incest was almost
too taboo a subject for them to bring up for discussion. They certainly
did not want to dwell on the details. Cathy said she believed the incest
occurred and knowing any more would not change the past or help
anyone:

> As far as the details are concerned, I don't want to know anything about it
> because I think that would give me a whole lot of emotional problems like,
> "How could she live with that? How could she deal with that and still go
> to school and everything?" She's already made it through that part, and so

has he, and me worrying and thinking about it isn't going to change the past. . . . It's just too painful to think about the details.

But once the incest was brought up, the mothers had no difficulty expounding on how they felt about it. Incest was wrong; it was horrible; it was serious.

David Finkelhor has made a cogent argument for why sex between adults and children is wrong. Children cannot give informed consent to participate in sex with an adult for they lack the necessary knowledge and power to make such a decision.[1] The mothers who spoke to me were unanimous and unequivocal in their judgment that incest was wrong.

Cathy spoke for all the mothers in her condemnation of sex between adults and children:

> It is absolutely, positively wrong for adults to have sex with children. No grey areas or anything else. It's just wrong. Children don't have any choice in the matter. Where it's two children experimenting, fine; two adults experimenting, they know what they're doing and they want to willingly be there. As far as adults and children go, that's wrong.

Freud asked, "What is the ultimate source of this horror [of incest]?"[2] Durkheim answered that the source of the horror lay in the blood taboo.[3] The degree of horror, fear, terror, or loathing that incest holds for a person will often depend on the blood tie. For some, sex between a stepfather and daughter is not as horrible as it would be between a biological father and his daughter, and for this reason stepdaughters may be more at risk of incest than biological daughters.[4]

The mothers who spoke to me were horrified about the incest beyond the blood tie. Ann's husband was the biological father, but for her the incest was horrible because it was so indefinable, so outside the realm of her reality. Her voice choked as she told me how she felt:

> I didn't know anything about such a situation. I had never encountered it. I didn't even know what to call it. I was horrified. It was such a taboo thing. Why, I didn't even know people bothered little children. . . . I cannot conceive of someone who can—to his own—oh! the things that they repeated to me. They said—I find it hard to relate to the pictures that come up of one man, someone that you think is great and you love and trust, and it's hard to understand they have the capacity for that. I just feel horrible about it.

Fay's daughter was sexually abused by her stepfather, but for Fay it was just as horrible because of the images she held of the sexual behavior between her husband and daughter. Like Ann, Fay's words were underlined with repugnance:

> It is a very sick thing. I'm sick about it. I'm disgusted. It makes me sick to think about my eleven-year-old daughter doing that. Oh! It just turns my stomach.

How serious is incest in relation to the other terrible things that can happen to a child? "Serious" infers the consequences of danger or harm. Ann was very forceful in her indictment of the incest as a sacrilege of the body.

> You know they say there's things worse than death, right? Well, that's where I categorize incest. Your body is the temple of your spirit and the Lord's spirit. And I feel then that nobody else can invade it. I guess because of my background, or downplaying one's body, or this protection of it—.

Bonnie vehemently declared incest to be the very worst kind of rape, the worst kind of abuse:

> Incest is the very worst thing that could happen—worse than physical abuse, psychological abuse, or neglect, because it is all of those. It was neglect of the parent role, a denial of love. Psychologically, her control of her self was destroyed, her feelings of what love was was destroyed. The base for her first male-female relationship was destroyed. It was worse than being raped by a stranger.

Ellen spoke of the memory of incest that could never be erased from the mind in the same way a physical beating could be:

> I had hundreds of beatings. I'll tell you something. A beating you can get over. Something like this is going to be in your mind forever. I can put what happened with my brothers behind me, but I'll never be able to forget it. You know, there's certain things you can forget, but something like this you just ain't never going to forget.

Fay, however, thought physical abuse was worse than incest. Physical abuse was more visible, something she would have seen, and therefore something that would have prompted her to act sooner.

> I would say this is probably the second most horrible thing that could happen to my daughter. I think physical abuse and to beat a child is a lot worse. Maybe not a lot, but quite a bit worse. This has got to be second on the scale. If she had been physically abused, we would have left a long time ago. I would have known about that. No, there's no way we would have ever stuck together.

There was no ambivalence among the mothers about how they defined and felt about the incest itself. It was wrong; it was horrible; it was serious. And their outrage resembled the social outrage we are witnessing today as the prevalence of incest in our society is being uncovered.

RESPONSES TO DAUGHTER

The mothers did not talk about their emotional responses to their daughters as spontaneously or as vividly as they did about their responses to the incest event itself. In general they did not talk about their daughters at all, particularly in regard to the incest, unless I asked a direct question. But what did surface was an absence of anger or blame and the presence of empathy.

If the mothers were angry at their daughters, they had difficulty expressing it directly. Ellen, who of all the mothers in this book had the most fragmented relationship with her daughter, insisted over and over again that she was not mad or angry at her for the incest that began when her daughter was three years old. She did, however, talk about the hurt and confusion she felt, because her daughter continued the sexual relationship with her father after she should have known it was wrong.

> Her willingness to allow the sexual relationship she was having with her father when she was old enough to try to stop it bewilders and hurts me. She knew the difference between right and wrong because I taught her right from wrong.

Cathy expressed a similar concern about her daughter.

> When she told me about the oral sex I told her, "You know that's wrong, don't you, honey? But I know it wasn't your fault."

Ellen and Cathy both held concrete ideas about what was right and wrong and focused on that rather than expressing any overt anger toward their daughters. On the surface it might even appear that they held their daughters responsible for stopping the sexual activity, and if this is so, it is as close as any of the mothers got to blaming their daughters for any part of the incest. The other mothers may have felt anger toward their daughters, but none expressed any part of this anger directly to me during our interviews.

In contrast to their inability to express anger, the mothers were able to express varying degrees of empathy toward their daughters. Both Fay and Cathy talked spontaneously about their feelings for the hurt their daughters experienced, almost as if they were taking on those feelings on behalf of their daughters. Fay said she was "overwhelmed":

> When I think of what that poor little girl had to go through, it's overwhelming. It's too hard for me to comprehend.

Cathy told me of the hurt she felt for her daughter and how she wanted to comfort her:

> I just—I felt really like somebody had hurt my baby. . . . I wanted to comfort her, just like if she falls down and gets hurt. I wanted to pick her up and love her and tell her it's okay.

For Bonnie, it was somewhat different. Bonnie needed her daughter to understand her hurt, to help her sort out her guilt and her part in the incest event. It will help us to understand Bonnie's reaction if we remember that her relationship with her daughter was in the peer mode while Cathy's and Fay's were in the parent-child mode. Bonnie talked about her need for her daughter:

> The night she told me I turned to my friend, and she went to a girlfriend's to spend the night. The next day I asked her to stay home from school. I just needed her there to help me sort it out—to help me to understand. And recently I told her. "We've got to talk." I needed her again to sort it out. . . . But she didn't want to talk about it. I remember we were driving and I said, "One of these days we've got to talk about it." And she said, "Mom, I told you I don't want to talk about it." And I said, "I understand your situation, but you've got to understand that I'm feeling pain from this, too." Oh, the pain of my involvement, my guilt; I've got to sort it out. And she just ran into the house crying.

When I questioned Bonnie more directly about her feelings toward her daughter, she spoke with deep empathy at first, but then her rational self stepped in.

> I feel pain. Oh, God! Overwhelming love to do everything I could to make it up to her. I can't give her back her childhood. . . . In a sense I denied her a mother's reaction. I became a very calculating, unemotional, responding adult to her. I didn't weep with her as a mother discovering what had happened. Now I'm realizing that was something I should have shown her, but at the time I felt very positive about the way I did handle it. I didn't cry with her though.

The interviews did not yield the depth of empathic responses I had originally expected from mothers whose daughters had experienced the hurt of incest. But I do not believe we can assume that a mother does not feel empathy for her daughter simply because she does not express overt concern. There may be a difference between what a mother actually feels and what she is able to express. First, some level of denial about the horror of incest may cover empathetic responses. A mother's own sense of guilt and responsibility about the incest may mask her caring responses to her daughter. And finally, the mother may be putting more energy into the expression of anger toward her husband and her protective behavior than into tapping and releasing her feelings for her daughter. Certainly daughters who fear, realistically or not, their mothers' disbelief, anger, or blame need understanding responses from their mothers. But for some mothers it may be necessary for them to first learn to identify their feelings and then how to express them.

RESPONSES TO HUSBAND

Margaret Myer found from the mothers' anger/empathy responses she recorded for her study, "The angrier [the mothers] are toward the offenders and the sexual abuse, the more likely they are to protect their children."[5]

All the mothers expressed some form of anger toward their husbands. Cathy's intitial anger toward her husband was mixed with her empathy for her daughter:

> I felt like somebody had hurt my baby and I was really mad at him. I was furious at him. I felt real protective toward my daughter, and I just hated him. How could he hurt her, emotionally as well as physically? How could he do that? And I just hated him. It took me two or three weeks to even talk to him. I couldn't go to the jail or anything. He would call me on the phone, and I would talk to him but I'd tell him I wasn't ready to deal with it. I just couldn't believe he would do that. I just hated him. I didn't want to be anywhere around him.

Bonnie said she had to mollify her anger in deference to what she projected her daughter's feelings to be:

> Anger was the first emotion that surfaced, but I had to temper it to keep her secret. I would have thrown him in jail. But she didn't want him to know. She told me she feared him. So I felt if she had kept the secret that long, she was probably saying, "It's still my secret. I've shared it with you. It's not your secret. You can't do what you want with it." A lot of this is me reading her thoughts because we've never discussed it.

Ann said the conflict between her anger and other values made it difficult for her to express her anger:

> I'm grappling with my faith to forgive and forgive and forgive and don't harbor anger. I have mixed feelings. You can be angry about something and want to get it out, but then there's always that threat hanging over you that if you do and it affects somebody so adversely, then you're responsible for their actions and their response to what you're getting out.

As Ellen talked, she began to put pieces of the past together:

> I figured, how low can a man go to do this sort of stuff to a little three-year-old kid? And then things started going off. Now I know why he wanted me working nights. Now I know why and it wasn't so we wouldn't have to pay a babysitter, and why my daughter and I had such a bad relationship. You know I was really getting bitter and mad at him.

Ellen and Diane were angry with their husbands because they "got away with it." Ellen's anger was still raw in her throat as she spoke:

> He got off scott free. The kid's admitting that the guy has done this to her since she was three years old! Why should he get off? I don't know what good it would do to throw him in jail either. But there should be some kind

of law. They should do something—castrate him so he can't do it to anybody else.

Diane was less vengeful but still bothered about the seeming lack
of justice:

> I don't think men should be allowed to get away with this. This is the one
> thing that bothers me now with my husband. I think he feels he got away
> with it. And in some instances he has.

Fay felt her husband was a man who was sick, needed help, and
ought to be punished, but she said she could not forgive him for what
he did to her daughter.

> It was a wrong and sick thing for him to do. I don't hate him for doing it.
> It's not like you would hate somebody. I don't feel that way. I'm sick about
> it. I'm disgusted. . . . I don't want to physically hurt him. . . . He needs help.
> I want him out of my life. I want him out of my daughter's life. He needs
> help, and he needs to be punished. . . . His mother would encourage me to
> forgive and forget. But I just can't forgive and forget.

When the mothers in Myer's study had empathic feelings for both
their husbands and their daughters, they were more ambivalent about
taking protective action, even when they sided with their daughters.[6]
The only mothers in this book who expressed any degree of empathy
toward their husbands, along with their anger, were Cathy and Diane,
who planned to reconcile with them. Yet, both sided with and took
strong protective action on behalf of their daughters. Cathy did not
support her husband during his arrest, conviction, and sentencing to a
prison term and Diane had forcibly evicted her husband from the home
through a Protection from Abuse Order. But while they both expressed
anger at their husbands, the anger faded in the face of other feelings for
them. Diane said that she just couldn't stop loving her husband and that
in many ways he was a good man:

> I can't say I've ever quit loving him. I've loved him for twenty-five years. I
> can't just turn that off and say, "Well, you did wrong, I don't love you no
> more." I sometimes wished I could have. I really do. There's times I've hated
> him, but basically speaking, I love him. Basically he's a very good person. I
> know this, and I hurt him terrible, but he's still felt his duties too. He provides
> support to me and the children in spite of the fact he's out of the home.

Cathy said that in the past year she had vented all her anger, still
loved her husband, and now wanted her family back together again:

> I've already dealt with all those angry feelings, and I don't have any real
> strong feelings toward nobody. The strongest feeling I have is wanting my
> family back together without the fear. . . . When my friends talk to me, they

say, "We can't believe you don't hate him. If that would have been me, I would have killed him. I'd never want to see him again." And I wondered about it. Why do I still feel like this? I still love him.

Richard Gelles, in his study of abused wives, suggests that a lack of economic, social, and emotional resources will keep women with or send them back to men who have mistreated them.[7] Cathy and Diane were in need of the economic resources their husbands provided, although both had found ways to support themselves and their children with their husbands out of the home. Cathy was receiving public assistance while her husband was in prison, and life was hard for her financially. But she never suggested that her husband's substantial paycheck would be a reason for wanting to reconcile with him.

Diane's husband was providing her with some financial support, but life was still difficult since she was not working. Diane did not want to believe she would take her husband back just for more money:

I'm still receiving unemployment. But it runs out very quickly here. This is one of the biggest problems for me right now, because when the unemployment runs out, I don't have a job. I've been looking, but there's nothing available. And I don't want to take him back because I think I can't live. It's a very pressing problem for me, that this is what's going to happen because there's no work. I'm trying to find work because at least then I won't feel I'm doing it for that reason.

The mothers had no difficulty expressing their anger toward their husbands. They believed their husbands should be punished for what they had done; and when they got away with it, as four fathers did, the mothers were doubly angry. The different levels of their anger may be related to the degree to which they feared their husbands. As we learned from them in the previous chapter, all of the mothers experienced some form of physical or psychological abuse. And as Suzanne Sgroi suggested, the absence or presence of this fear may be a crucial dynamic in the ability of a mother to protect her daughter.[8] We now turn to the different ways the mothers actually behaved in response to the disclosure of incest.

The Mothers' Behavioral Responses

The emotional reactions of the mothers in this book did not necessarily pave the way to protective action, and the way each mother responded to the incest was unique to her own situation. In this section I will look at the mothers' behavioral responses in terms of four categories: no protective action necessary, immobilization, attempted action thwarted, and protective action taken.

NO PROTECTIVE ACTION NECESSARY

Bonnie and Ellen learned of the incest event after they had divorced their husbands. It was not necessary for either of them to provide protection for their daughters, but their stories raise certain questions about what a mother should do after she learns about the incest. What kinds of things does a mother say to her daughter following disclosure? How does she go about helping her daughter to recover from the trauma of incest? How does she insure her daughter's future protection? Can she do all this alone?

Bonnie's daughter told her about the incest a year and a half after it had stopped. The cessation of the incest corresponded with Bonnie leaving and divorcing her husband because he had started to physically abuse one of her younger sons. Bonnie remembers saying "all the right things" to her daughter:

> I said all the right things. I became a very calculating, unemotional, responding adult to her. I handled myself the way I handle rape victims and mothers of rape victims. I said all the right things as a disinterested third party.

Bonnie went on to question her daughter about when the incest began, how often it occurred, the kind of sexual behavior that took place, and whether it had happened since her separation from her husband. Bonnie said her controlled emotional detachment made this kind of questioning possible, whereas other mothers reported that the incest was so painful they could not even think about it and avoided asking for any details.

While protective action was not necessary, Bonnie took her daughter to a counselor and made provisions to protect her daughter in the future. She talked about her fear of dying and leaving her daughter unprotected:

> When I first found out about my daughter and everything and I was studying the options on how to handle it—one thing that I found being a single parent. Boy! Do I fear my dying. In fact, the night I found out I called my brother. I instantly wanted someone to be acting in my stead. If I had an accident, I wanted my brother to know and fight tooth and nail that my husband would not be with my daughter. We were going to have her write in her own words what happened. This was my idea. I wanted her own words in her own handwriting, notarized and attached to my will, so that if I were to die, and she suddenly came up with this story, it would not appear as a late concoction, just to avoid being with her dad or something. Well, she just never wrote that. She just never would write it, so we don't have her statement.

In this situation disclosure of the incest was private; thus, no official outsiders were involved with Bonnie and her daughter. Bonnie was able, on her own, to elicit information from her daughter about the incest, but she was unable, by herself, to ensure ongoing counseling for her.

Nor was her daughter willing to talk to her about the incest on later occasions. The only court action Bonnie took was around custody to ensure that her ex-husband had no further contact with her daughter.

Ellen's situation was somewhat different. Ellen's daughter had been living with her father, who had gained custody of her when her parents divorced five years earlier. After seeing a television program on incest, Ellen's daughter told the police her father had been sexually abusing her since she was three years old. The county Children and Youth Services Agency intervened and placed Ellen's daughter in a foster home and called Ellen, who had remarried and was living in another state. Ellen related what she said to her daughter after she was under the jurisdiction of a protective agency:

> I talked to her on the phone that day. I told her I wasn't mad at her, and I said a lot of things had been answered in my mind, and I know now that the things that happened weren't all her fault. We had to go up two days later to court. When I saw my daughter, she ran over and put her arms around me. I put my arms around her and hugged her back. I said I didn't want her to feel guilty the rest of her life because of what happened. I explained that what had happened to her had happened to me, only different. Ya, I told her, and she about flipped. I didn't ask her anything about what he had done. She volunteered it.

Ellen was unable to provide a home for her daughter. The Children and Youth Services Agency gained custody and provided protection, foster care, and counseling. Ellen began having visits with her daughter. However, Ellen, who had felt so alienated from her daughter for so long, was unable to make any kind of an emotional reconnection with her. Geographic distance, Ellen's current family situation, and her deep sense of estrangement from her daughter made it difficult for her to be a part of her daughter's healing process. On one occasion her daughter asked her to attend one of her therapy sessions. Ellen described her feelings about this experience:

> My feelings about my daughter's doctor are that she is a so-called professional who wants to show her authority but does not have the capability of compassion at the same time, at least for me. I realize my daughter is her patient, and they are working together, but it was her attitude toward me that I feel she lacked understanding. . . . She made me feel baffled and badgered at the same time. She made me feel like she was infallible and that I knew nothing of what I was saying—about anything! When she kept insisting I had a problem about my daughter's part in the incest and I'd try to explain, I was never given the opportunity to finish an explanation. . . . I also felt the doctor's occasional little quips about my parental judgment in front of my daughter was uncalled for. If she had asked my daughter about my judgment instead of telling her, it would have been a more professional manner.

It was clear that Ellen felt alienated and alone. She needed understanding and help for herself before she would be able to participate in her daughter's healing process. Ellen told me how she was still struggling to feel reconnected to her daughter:

> Every day I try to feel closer to my daughter, but I can't. I guess it's because she doesn't keep in close contact with me. I write her letters, and I wait for weeks to get an answer. Even when she comes to visit, I can't get close. I try, I really do. She is very distant. We are always on the offensive with each other. I guess she feels I am the enemy. When she was living with her father, I felt that way about her. I don't anymore. I don't feel any malice toward her, but it's hard to define what I feel. I guess to use the word "limbo" would best describe it.

Because disclosure of the incest was public this time, outsiders were involved. While Ellen was able to respond supportively to her daughter, "outsiders" provided for and met the ongoing needs of her daughter: living arrangements, counseling, and protection from further abuse by the father, which Ellen, by herself, had been unable to provide in the past.

It is not always necessary for a mother to take protective action after disclosure, as was the case with Bonnie and Ellen. But protective action extends beyond physical protection to helping a daughter to heal from the trauma of incest and working to strengthen the mother-daughter bond. Bonnie and Ellen illustrated some of the mother-daughter issues still present among incest-families where post-disclosure protective action by the mother is not necessary.

IMMOBILIZATION

Margaret Myer characterized four mothers in her study who were immobilized by the situation and unable to take any protective action on behalf of their daughters as "inadequate mothers and women who had a diagnosis of borderline personalities."[9] I use the term "immobilized," however, in a different way than Myer's diagnostic interpretation.

Ann was immobilized from taking action beyond confronting her husband after the incest was accidentally disclosed. While Ann typifies what a mother's perceptions and options might have been in the 1950s, her reactions may be similar to those of some mothers even today. Ann's own reaction to what she had discovered was quite different from her husband's. She tried to explain to me what happened to her inside as her husband "rationalized" her out of taking any further steps:

> I didn't know anything about such a situation. I had never encountered it. I didn't even know what to call it. I had been assured that my daughter would be all right because nothing really serious had happened between my daughter and my husband. He asked to be forgiven. It would never happen again. He

said the police would say he had done something if I called them or the doctor. I was rationalized out of doing anything. I was told I was overreacting. . . . But something had happened to me, and I had that awful feeling that something just turned over, and I knew it was never going to turn back again. But I really believed that was the end of it, and I had overreacted simply because I didn't understand.

Ann said she wanted to reach out for help, wanted to tell someone:

I never got over the feeling of wanting to talk to somebody about it. And I did get to the point of calling my doctor because I really had exploded all over. I was going to call the police and everything. I just went off my guard about it. But my husband said it really wasn't anything, that others wouldn't believe it, and this was just a lot of fuss about nothing, that it wouldn't be understood and would break up the family, or maybe it was that they'd take the children away from me or something. But I did calm down, reasoning with myself that it was me. It was inside me. And when I did call the doctor, he thought I was calling him about having a play center at the house, and all of a sudden he sort of brought me back to reality and I thought, "Well, I have to deal with these other things, and this may not be as big as I think it is." And that was that.

Ann continued to talk about her shock, her confusion, and to examine her feelings and responses and why she did not do something:

Right in the beginning my courage was at its utmost because I was so shocked and so angry about hearing that anything like this could happen. I didn't know what it was, and I guess I was so horrified. Why, I didn't know that people bothered little children, and I guess that was my opportunity to follow through and call someone and do something. And why didn't I do it? Just to say this has happened, and what can I do? What should I do? There isn't always the right someone to tell. When you go to someone, you take your chances. I couldn't even go out to find a book even. It was such a taboo thing, so frightening. I felt such a sense of threat. I had such an uncertainty in my own judgment. From where I am today, I cannot understand why I didn't follow through. That was a perfect example of someone talking me out of doing something. I assume my first reaction was probably the right one. And why was I the kind of person that could be put in a box of fear like that and shut up?

Ann tried to understand what might have contributed to her inability to act at the time of disclosure. She continued to examine her tendency to overreact to things, particularly sexual things, but could not shake the guilt about having done nothing at the time of her discovery:

I was in a position to do something and I didn't. That really lays on me. I should have talked to somebody, but was I overreacting? I was led to believe I was. Everybody else was all right. It was just me that wasn't all right. My knowledge and perception as far as the physical and sexual were concerned, that was probably lopsided. I mean, that was always my fear, that I over-reacted. I remember spending time at one of my aunt's, and she was going to give me a bath, and I was just terrified of taking all my clothes off and having anyone touch me. And later you find out in life that doesn't happen to very many people, but by and large that's an overreaction due to programming.

Ann's story illustrates one mother's immobility, not because she was necessarily inadequate, but because she was confused. Ann lacked confidence in her own feelings about what had happened as well as her own judgment about what to do. And so her husband, who defined the situation as not really serious, was able to talk her out of doing anything. In addition, Ann was not only uninformed about sexual behavior in general, but the idea of sex between adults and children was, in her mind, beyond the realm of possibility. There was little if any information about incest or child sexual abuse available, and few trusted people to whom she could turn in the 1950s. Ann did not even have the concepts or vocabulary to frame the questions she had. But today she knows she was not overreacting; she was not the one who was distorting the situation.

ATTEMPTED PROTECTIVE ACTION THWARTED

It would be difficult to estimate how many incest-family mothers have attempted to take some kind of protective action when they suspected that their daughters were incest victims, action that may have been thwarted in some way. Ellen told me how she discovered her daughter at age three involved in oral sex play with her five-year-old brother and two other children around the same ages:

> There they were, all engaged in oral sex. And without trying to blow my top, and without trying to make them feel that—because of all the stuff you read, I mean that you shouldn't make a child feel that it's dirty. And I'm figuring this out in my head. I just tried very calmly to send the other kids home and tried to get to the bottom of what was going on, because this was not normal. They had to see it somewhere. Kids this age do not investigate that kind of stuff on their own. They play doctor and what-have-you. But not oral sex.

Ellen knew she needed to do something, so she called her doctor, who said the children's sex play was "perfectly normal." Ellen said she did not agree.

> So I called my family doctor and he said that's perfectly normal and I told him right out—I said, "Well, doctor." I said, "For three- and five-year-old kids, oral sex is not normal." And then I called the mother of the other kids, and she got all bent out of shape, saying that I had a dirty mind and blah, blah, blah. So I tried to work it all out.

Initially, Ellen made no connection between the sex play and possible incest between her husband and daughter. On another occasion, shortly after her daughter had chosen to live with her father, friends reported their "adult lover" behavior to her. Ellen again suspected something, and this time she said she did make a connection, and she made another call:

> Friends would say they looked like lovers walking up the street holding hands. And he would put his arm around her. My sister told me that when they'd come to visit her, my daughter would sit in his lap and blow kisses in his ear, and stuff like that. So I went to the school. My kids went to Catholic school, and I went to the nun who was the principal and told her what I thought was happening. We got hold of Child Protective Services. I thought something screwy was going on. So CPS came and interviewed the kid. My daughter wouldn't say anything. And it just made me look like I was making this all up. So I dropped it. I tried to talk to my daughter about it. I tried to say it without saying it, but she wouldn't open up.

This particular incident illustrates that a mother may see the signs, become suspicious, attempt to take action, and then be thwarted by people and circumstances beyond her control.

PROTECTIVE ACTION TAKEN

Kirson Weinberg states that only a minority of mothers are capable of forceful, protective action, because most mothers are so passive and intimidated by the father.[10] David Finkelhor has even suggested that incest-family mothers are "natural scapegoats":

> These women are better visualized as victims themselves than as culprits. They are often physically beaten or otherwise intimidated by their husbands. More importantly, like so many women in our society, they are trapped by their economic and social position.[11]

In addition, Suzanne Sgroi notes that many mothers lack the resources to protect their daughters alone:

> Few mothers have the strength or resources to accomplish [protective action] by themselves. Many mothers fear change, shrink from separation, dread retribution by the perpetrator, and shirk or feel inadequate to perform tasks and fulfill the responsibilities to stop the incest.[12]

Yet, despite fear and intimidation and a lack of resources, two studies clearly show that mothers are capable of protective action. Janet Gilgun reported, "In none of the families did the mother fail to take action when the [sexual] abuse was disclosed."[13] Further, over half the mothers Myer studied took action to protect their daughters, and over half of that group acted without any ambivalence in choosing their daughters over their husbands. Myer concluded that what made the difference between the two groups of mothers was their anger/empathy balance in regard to their daughters and husbands. If they were empathetic to their husbands, their protective responses tended to be more ambivalent, and their need for pressure from outside authorities was greater.[14]

Cathy, Diane, and Fay took action to protect their daughters after disclosure, but it was difficult to organize their behavior into "without ambivalence" or "with ambivalence" categories. The ways in which these mothers defined their options seemed to go beyond the dichotomous husband versus daughter choice. Instead, the protective action any mother does or does not take is better seen and understood within a social context, which includes the state of the marriage before disclosure and the involvement of outsiders at the time of disclosure.

According to Myer's typology, Cathy and Diane were ambivalent in that they were empathic to their husbands as well as their daughters, and when they spoke with me they were planning to reconcile with their husbands. But this alone did not appear to be significantly related to whether they took action or not.

Cathy did not feel ambivalent about the choice she had to make between her husband and her daughter. But she described how she was pulled in different directions by different factions representing her daughter and her husband:

> I felt like I was in the middle of a wheel, and everybody was pulling at me from different ways. Children's Services wanted me to be all on the girls' side and forget about him. His parents wanted me to be on his side and say, "Well, it wasn't his fault. Keep it quiet. Cover everything up." Well, I'm not going to sweep it under the rug or hide my head under the pillow. I couldn't know that one of my kids was being hurt and allow it to continue. I just couldn't. I'd seen that program "Quincy." It was about incest. The mother knew about it while it was happening and allowed it to continue. I just couldn't understand that. That's what I couldn't accept.

In the end Cathy's choice was more a conciliation between her husband and her daughter in the service of the marriage. But she insisted she was still protecting her daughter:

> I had to step back and think about what I really wanted. Okay, what do I expect to happen now? What is the most important thing to me? Do I want to say, that's it? My marriage is over and done, there's going to be no more family here?" The more I thought about it, the more I knew that what I wanted was for him to get the help that he needed with his drinking and to put our life back together if it was possible. Now, if he didn't want it, or if he wanted to continue the way he was, then there's no sense in trying. But as long as he wanted to try, then I wanted to.

Cathy tried to explain how her daughter felt about the choice she made, and how she stood her ground:

The girls could not believe that I was making that choice, that I was making them have that choice. It was either they could have me along with their father, or they could just leave, and I said, "You don't understand from my point of view. I chose your father to spend the rest of my life with. You are my kids. You are my responsibility, but sooner or later you are going to grow up and have a new life of your own, and I'll still be your mother, but you will go on with your life." They saw me choosing him over them, but I was trying to help him as much as I was trying to help them, because he thought like he was locked away and deserted, and nobody cared about him, and I wanted him to know that I still cared, that he was still important to me. I've told them the most important thing to me is having our family back together.

Diane was also ambivalent about choosing between her husband and daughter but talked about it more directly and appeared to be more clear about her choices:

I think at the time this happened, it's one of the hardest things for the woman because she's the one that has to decide between the daughter and the husband. I made up my mind I was going to protect my daughter and myself at any cost.

Researchers and clinicians often get caught up in the situation at a particular moment in time, forgetting that things have happened before that moment that may influence the course of events. The context of the marital and family situation before disclosure appeared to contribute to the different kinds of protective action Fay and Cathy took.

Fay described her marriage as a mistake from the beginning. She said the incest was the last straw for a marriage built on a lie and riddled with problems during its four-year duration:

I feel I have been kicked around for four years with a person who really didn't give a damn. He didn't care about the welfare of her or me. The whole time I was married, I knew I was never going to be happy with this guy. I told myself, "You're never going to get anywhere financially, emotionally—this guy is not right for you." And the whole four years it's been a battle on my mind. Now all marriages are brought together from the Lord, and I believe that this is one of them that had not been brought together under the Lord's eyes. This is a mistake in my life, and this is my way that I must correct it. Just get my divorce and start all over again.

Fay went on to speculate how it might be more difficult for a woman who loved her husband to protect her daughter:

This would be hard for a woman who loves a man. Maybe that's why a lot of women can't admit it happened, can't believe their daughter. They feel more threatened because they want this marriage, they love their husbands, and they don't want this to happen. It might have been easier for me because

I knew he had a lot of problems, and several times when I wanted to leave him, I knew he needed help with other situations, and I knew he wasn't the best of fathers or the best of husbands. I knew I didn't totally love him. That probably helped me more than it does a lot of other women who really love their husbands.

Cathy also experienced marital difficulties before she learned about the incest and had been prepared to separate from her husband:

Before this happened I was ready to leave him. I was sick and tired of him drinking all the time, and I would ask different people, "How can I force him to leave?" It was too hard for me to try to find a place that I could afford on what I was making. I just couldn't afford it. So it would be a lot easier if he would just take his truck and TV and leave.

But even though the idea of separating from her husband was not new to Cathy, and she had already thought about how she would make it without him, Cathy continued to love him and felt she had to consider the whole family rather than just her daughter or her husband. She did not waver, however, from the protective action she had to take on behalf of her daughter when the time came.

Cathy's husband did not deny the incest accusation, the authorities had removed him from the home, and Cathy's protective action meant not bailing him out—literally and figuratively. Cathy described what happened after her husband was arrested:

When I called his parents to say he had been arrested and he might be calling them for bail, I said, "I don't want you to post bail for him," because at that time I wanted the girls to know that they could trust me, that I was going to help them. I was going to help them.

Cathy also resisted her husband's pleas to help him:

He put pressure on me in the beginning. He wanted me to go to the lawyer, talk to the lawyer, get his sentence reduced, go to the judge, that kind of thing. I told him, "I can't do that. I don't feel comfortable in doing that. You know, like you got yourself in trouble, and you expect me to get you out. I can't do that just because I want you to be home."

In contrast to Cathy's situation, Diane's husband did deny the incest allegation, and Diane's behavior was responsive to both the action of the authorities and her husband's denial. Following Diane's report to the authorities, her daughter was removed from the home but was returned when Diane guaranteed she would provide 24-hour surveillance for her daughter. Diane told me what happened:

I couldn't give it [protection] to her [while he was still in the house]. He would get up at night. You cannot be up day and night. And if he started prowling at night, though he never went to her room in that period, I was still afraid that he would, and for my peace of mind I had to put my husband out, forcibly. It was something you have to do. You have to keep him away from your daughter.

Diane admitted she had needed the ongoing encouragement and support from professionals with authority to reinforce and help her to sustain her protective action in the face of her vulnerability to her husband's definition of the situation:

At one point in the game it got so bad for me that I think I really felt—well, my husband kept telling me I was crazy to begin with, and at one point in the game I really felt I was. And everything I was going through was part of a crazy pattern that I had connived in my mind, and he really hadn't done nothing. But Rape Crisis explained to me that there were five charges; it wasn't all in my head. You get to the point where you don't know what's real and what isn't. I had begun to think that somehow because he had always said I was crazy, maybe I was. And maybe I was making this all up, and that none of it had taken place at all. At one point I thought I'd actually gone insane; that nothing really made sense; that this was all part of my insanity. And through Rape Crisis and my caseworker from Children's Services and my psychologist, I finally did get myself straightened out where I realize now I'm not crazy. This has happened, and he did commit these crimes. It is a crime. It's not just a little misdemeanor I've built up in my head. It took a long time to get myself to come around. And then I think I finally started to accept things. I refused to let him rule me.

Diane's lack of confidence in her own perceptions of reality resemble Ann's fear of overreacting. But Diane had the support of outsiders who helped her to have confidence in her construction of reality, and this helped her to follow through with her protective action.

Fay, the third mother who took protective action, was much more certain about her definition of the situation. She told me she had no difficulty knowing who was at fault and who was sick:

After she told what had happened, I told her I loved her, and I am by her side. I was sorry that this happened, and it wasn't her fault. It was his fault. He's sick, and there's something terribly wrong with him, and I'm going to call the police and have him arrested, and we're going to split our family up.

Fay initiated protective action and was able to act without any pressure or need for any reinforcement or support from outside professionals with authority. She described how she actively involved them in her determined action to protect her daughter.

First I called Children's Services and reported it. I thought they'd give me some advice over the telephone, just kind of to get my head straight. When I explained what had happened, they were great. They gave me an ear. They listened, and I told them, "I want him out of my house. I do not want this guy in my house anymore. Can you help me out?" And she said, "Oh, it's going to be hard to get him arrested and get him out of the house. It could take a couple of days." I said, "I'll take care of it" and hung up and called the police and made an appointment for the next day to go down and issue a warrant.

Fay told me she faced her husband with her knowledge that very night:

My husband was at work, and when he came home, he didn't know anything about this, but I confronted him that night. I told him I knew what happened between him and my daughter, and I said, "I know you're going to deny this, but I'm going to tell you I know about it. I know what you did. I know the whole story. Do you know you can really physically injure a little girl like that for her whole life? Her insides could be ruined because of what you did." And he just looked at me and said, "Did what?" like he didn't know. He was denying it. I expected that, but I just said, "Fine" and dropped it. I didn't want to cause any trouble because he would just deny it, and we'd end up in a big fight.

The following day Fay carried out her plan, giving her daughter support and encouragement every step of the way:

The next day I took my daughter to the police station, and she told them the whole story. After she told the police, I told her, "Honey, I couldn't have done it that good." I told her I was proud of her. I said, "Honey, you're going to have to tell it to a few other people, but I'm going to be with you. You're just great". . . . The police issued out a warrant. I told them my husband comes home from work at six that evening, I would not be there, and when he gets home to please pick him up, and they did. And within twenty-four hours his mother bailed him out. . . . After I heard he was bailed out, I put deadlocks on the door with slide bolts because I felt that if he went out and got drunk and got real ugly—.

But Fay's protective action did not end with providing physical safety within her home:

After I went to the police, I called the doctor and made an appointment for my daughter that day. He thoroughly examined her, and I had him take a blood test to make sure she didn't have VD.

The presence of outsiders at the time of disclosure not only affected the kind of protective action a mother took but the effectiveness of her action as well. For example, Ann and Diane (in the first incident with her older daughter) discovered the incest, confronted their husbands, and trusted and believed that would be enough. Ann was talked out of taking any further action by her husband. But Diane was not immobilized and was able to confront her husband with more confidence in her own judgment than Ann was. As Diane told me:

> I sent her to bed, and then I told him that I didn't want it to ever happen again or that he would be out. I didn't go to any officials. It was strictly between us. And he said it wouldn't; it would never happen again. But he never said he was sorry. Then I talked to my daughter. She said it had only gone on a very short time. Then I told her I had stopped it. And it did stop. I asked her after if he was trying anything, and she said, "No."

Diane's husband did stop molesting this daughter but went on to molest a younger daughter. For Diane, confronting her husband, no matter how confidently, was not enough, not this time.

Several years later Diane began to suspect that her husband may have been abusing her youngest daughter. This time she told her therapist, which set the wheels in motion for the authorities to become involved:

> And then she told me I had to report it to Children's Services; that if I didn't, she would have to. . . . She finally did convince me that I should tell.

Support or pressure from outside authorities sometimes made it easier for a mother to initiate and follow through with protective action. It also made a mother's choices easier. Cathy learned of the incest when the police came to the house to arrest her husband. She wondered what she might have done if her daughter had told her directly instead of going to the police:

> If she would have told me, it would have been up to me to protect her, to do what was right for her, and it would have been me that would have to press the charges against him. Her going to the police, that was all taken out of my hands. But if I had to, I would have. If I had to choose sides, I would have done that. And because of the way I felt at the time, about not wanting to live like that anymore [with her husband's heavy drinking], it would have been easier just to say, "That's it. I don't want to talk about it; I don't care what you have to say. I don't want to hear it." But this way I don't feel like it was up to me to press the issue, to force it to happen, to take care of it.

Cathy said she felt it was also better for her husband that her daughter told someone outside the family:

> Yes, I would have called the police, but I don't think I could have even tried to go and talk to him or anything else. I would have called the police and said, "Come and get him. Take him away." I think that would have been the end of it. And that would have been worse. That would have been the end of everything. Because I think I would have felt more divided, that he would have blamed her. "Why did you have to go tell your mother?" And if he had

done that, I would have felt like he was just going to continue to let it be a deep, dark secret, and continue to lie to me. I just wouldn't feel like I could trust him.

The kinds of protective action a mother took, her reasons for taking it, and the effectiveness of her action seemed to be related to two factors. First was the state of the marriage before the disclosure of the incest. If the mother defined the marriage as a sham with no foundation, as Fay did, there was no ambivalence in choosing to support her daughter, and the disclosure of incest only served to reinforce a previously considered decision to end the marriage. Second was the involvement of outsiders. For Cathy, Diane, and Fay, disclosure of the incest was public and they received support from professional authorities to sustain their protective action.

Three additional factors also appeared to influence and shape the kinds of protective action a mother was able to take. These were her coping skills, her problem-solving abilities, and the availability and extent of her personal and family support networks.

Coping Skills

Coping skills refer to the ways a person reacts to and adapts to new situations. The mothers did not all react to disclosure or cope with the crisis of incest in the same ways; they contended with the disclosure of the incest with different coping styles and mechanisms. Diane simply did what she had to do; she put one foot in front of the other and utilized the help of the professionals around her. Fay actively acted on her environment, seeking out professionals to make things happen. But Cathy coped in a different way. She said she just wanted to be left alone to adjust to the situation:

> I wanted to go home and be by myself. I deal with things that are real traumatic better by myself than I do talking to a lot of people. I don't want to talk. I want to stop and think, and I want to be left alone to do it.

Cathy explained that in order to do what she had to do she could not think about the details of the incest:

> I know in general what went on and I don't want to think about it because it's too painful, and that's why I can deal with it—because I don't dwell on the details, just on what the problem was and how to make it better, how to work through it.

Cathy said she did not seek or want the advice of others but had confidence in her own levelheadedness:

> I think I'm pretty levelheaded and that's pretty important. You have to be

pretty well balanced in order to roll with the punches, not blowing up at everything, not overreacting to everything.

So Cathy coped by putting the problem away for a while:

> I can think about a problem but if I don't decide anything or come to any final decision, I can put it away in a little box for a while, and close the door on it and think about something else. I'll take it out later and say, "Okay, now I can look at it freshly."

Much of Cathy's behavior could have been misinterpreted by the professionals working with her. Not wanting to talk about the incest and wanting to be alone, not overreacting, and putting the problem away could have been construed as denial. But for Cathy they were functional coping mechanisms.

Problem Solving

Problem solving is the sequence of behaviors a person performs in response to a perceived difficulty or problem. Cathy and Fay described a sequence of thoughtfully planned steps to resolve the crisis of disclosure of the incest event. Fay's purposefully carried-out protective action has already been described. Cathy recounted the stages she went through in solving the problem as she experienced it. First were her emotional responses:

> The very first thing was I didn't believe it. It just can't be. The second thing, I just hated it. I was furious. I didn't want anything to do with him. I didn't want to talk to him again. I didn't want to see him because he hurt my babies. The third thing was I blamed him. "How could you do this to me?" Because he hurt me by hurting my kids.

Then Cathy logically went through a problem-solving process:

> The next step was thinking about what I really wanted. Just kinda stepping back and looking at it and saying, "Okay, what do I expect to happen now? What is the most important thing to me? Do I want to say, okay, that's it. My marriage is over and done? There's going to be no more family here?" The more I thought about it, the more I knew what I wanted was for him to get the help that he needed with the drinking and everything and to put our life back together if it was possible. Now, if he didn't get it, or he wanted to continue the way he was, then there was no sense in trying. But as long as he wanted to try, then I wanted to.

For Cathy the problem was not the end of the world or their lives. It was just something they would have to work through. Cathy had some idea how to do that and had confidence that she could do it.

Cathy was also creative in her problem solving. She told me how she reframed an issue she had to face in order to find a solution to a serious living problem:

> I think one of the hardest things for me to do after he was arrested was going to apply for assistance. That was because of the way him and I were both brought up. People on assistance were too lazy to go to work, because that's the way it was then. Jobs were plentiful, and if you didn't go out and get a job, it was just because you were too lazy. It's completely different today. A lot of people who had worked for years and years are being laid off, and they have nothing else. One woman I know lost her house to a sheriff's sale because she was laid off and couldn't make her mortgage payments and she was too proud to go and apply for assistance. And I thought about this problem. I would not go and apply for assistance because I didn't want to sign a lien against my house. That was really important to me. So I thought about, "What choices do I have? I can be like my friend and starve to death." You know, she came down to a point of either feeding her kids and paying the utilities or paying the mortgage. And I thought, "If it has to be, it has to be. Isn't a lien against my house better than losing it completely?" So I wrote to my husband and said, "I think we've been looking at this all wrong because when we wanted to buy the truck, we didn't think anything at all about going to a bank for a loan and we were paying twelve percent interest on that loan. So this is an interest-free loan. I'm saying to them that I need this money to pay my mortgage payment, but when I sell my house, I'll pay it back. But we don't have to wait that long. When you come out and are working, and I'm working, we can pay it off. We don't have to have that lien against the house if we don't want it. So really, we just don't like the name of this loan company because it's Public Assistance."

The mothers I interviewed exhibited different styles of problem solving. Some were able to figure out a problem or would know where to go to find the information necessary to do so. Some mothers were analytical in their approach, asking, "Is it solvable?" and looking at all the options. Others were more crisis oriented and impulsive in their behavior. Still others took direct action, planning each step, but acted quickly, almost impulsively, without a lot of thinking about alternative actions. And some mothers still needed the support and direction from outsiders to do what they knew needed to be done.

Isolation/Support Networks

The third factor related to the mothers' capacity to take protective action was their isolation/support network balance. The incest-family has been variously described as "isolated and withdrawn from society as a whole[15] and without regular contact with relatives, friends, and neighbors.[16] Isolation can be a physical construct or a state of mind. None of the mothers with whom I spoke described themselves as isolated in a physical sense. However, they did describe themselves as being either loners or seekers of help; trustful or mistrustful of community agencies and professional helpers; alone or with support networks available.

Ann was unable to articulate the problem of incest and, while a seeker of help, felt very alone in that she did not know how to tell anyone about the problem. Bonnie, on the other hand, reached out to talk to anyone available in her personal circles but said she would not use social service agencies, not only because she had a personal support network, but because she was reaslistic about the support she perceived she would get from society:

> If I were raped, I don't think I would call Rape Aid, and I don't think I would tell the police. Let's pretend that my daughter told her kindergarten teacher. My husband was a man of authority in the community. And the teacher may have known that. I don't think she would have called the Hotline. The teacher would be worried about what the repercussions of reporting would be— punishment of some sort, a law suit.

Fay described receiving active support from her family after the disclosure of the incest:

> Then I called my sister and cried to her and told her what happened. And that night I called my mother and told her what had happened. I said, "Mom, I need you to come down here. I need somebody." And you know, she did come. She came on the airplane and it was just a blessing that she could be here and help me through all this.

Cathy was resentful of the way professionals moved in on her, telling her what to do, and how to act, particularly in regard to her behavior with her children, but she did have family to turn to.

Initially, Diane felt very alone, with no sense of where to turn for help, not knowing whom to trust. She told me she couldn't even find any information to help her, particularly about mothers:

> For one thing, there is no information to help mothers. I've tried to get information. Most of it is very technical though and not in a language most mothers could understand. Mostly there was nothing that could give me comfort at a very trying time. I found that there was very litle comfort from anybody in this field for the mother in the beginning.

Eventually Diane found and did welcome the support and assistance she received from professional helpers in the community, even though she still defined herself as very much alone, even at the time of my interview with her.

Ellen, because of her past experiences, saw community social services as very supportive and helpful:

> I've had lots of experience with social workers. I think they're nice people. The first social worker I ever had anything to do with was when I went into a foster home, and she was like a mother to me, and she tried to find me a

home that would be suitable for me. And I had really good people in the mental health clinic.

Ellen explained how she advised her sister to use the helping people available to her:

> I just talked to my sister the other night. She told me my brother-in-law was taking pictures of his stepdaughter in the bathtub with her hands across her chest. I asked if she thought he ever fooled around with her, and she said she didn't think so. But I talked to the kid outright and told her that if her father ever fools around with her, please tell someone. Don't keep it to herself. . . . My sister says she can't get help from anyone. And I don't buy that. She can get help. I did. She says she don't know where to go or who to go to. I said, "You have a child who's going to speech class. And you have a social worker working with you. Talk to her. She'll tell you where to go, what agencies to go to. If they can't help, they'll direct you to someone who can."

The whole issue of incest-family mothers' ability to protect their daughters after disclosure has been clouded by misperceptions and erroneous conclusions about their behavior. There were different levels of protective behavior among the mothers in this book. It was not necessary for Bonnie and Ellen to protect their daughters from continued incest. Ann was immobilized, not because she was inadequate, but because her husband made her question her own sense of reality. Today, with the proliferation of information about incest and the publicized help available, there may not be as many mothers who would be as naive and as uninformed as Ann described herself, but we cannot be sure that there are not still some mothers in similar situations. Ellen attempted to protect her daughter when she first suspected incest, but her protective action was misinterpreted and thwarted by those to whom she turned. Cathy, Diane, and Fay were able to take protective action on behalf of their daughters, but not without a lot of help supporting their actions.

Several factors seemed to be related to the mothers' behavioral responses. First, the strength of the mothers' protective action appeared to be independent of any ambivalence they may have felt about having to choose between their husbands and daughters, although the state of the marriage before disclosure did appear to influence the purposefulness of the mothers' protective action.

Second, the support and pressure from outside authorities may have helped the mothers to initiate and sustain their protective action. This is an important finding since it has been speculated that intervention by outside authorities, while mandated and well meaning, only contributes to the family disruption following disclosure. Such an interpretation may impede decisive action and sap the confidence of less-experienced and untrained workers responsible for investigating and helping incest-families through the crisis period. Persons mandated to report suspected incest are also reluctant to do so because they often cannot see beyond the family chaos rising out of the crisis of disclosure.

Finally, the mothers' styles and skills of coping, their history of problem solving, and the presence of available support networks along with their ability to use them may have influenced the kinds of action they did or did not take, and the degree to which they could sustain such action.

In conclusion to this chapter, it is important to emphasize that in addition to each mother's individual strengths, resources, and potential to protect her daughter, their immediate social environments, as well as society at large, also shaped and influenced the ways in which they acted in response to the disclosure of the incest event.

We now turn to the different ways the mothers in this book explained what happened.

SIX

Explanations

I don't fully understand why it happened in
this family.

(Diane)

Reasons

Various explanations for incest have been offered from individual, family
systems, and social perspectives. Judith Herman has pointed out that
causal explanations for incest have been tied to individual responsibility
and over time have shifted from the pathological father to the seductive
daughter to the collusive mother.[1] Jon Conti has reviewed some of the
more "popular views" about the etiology of incest rooted in family systems dynamics: poor marital relations, particularly husband-wife sexual
estrangement; role reversal between the mother and daughter; and a
perversely ingrown family system with the mother as the "cornerstone"
in the family pathology leading to incest.[2] And more recently a feminist
analysis has set incest within the context of a patriarchal society.[3] Judith
Herman proposes a patriarchal family hypothesis:

> In any culture, the greater the degree of male supremacy and the more rigid
> the sexual division of labor, the more frequently one might expect the taboo
> on father-daughter incest to be violated.[4]

While feminists have rallied around this theory that incest "occurs more
frequently in families characterized by extreme [male] dominance,"[5] such
a theory has yet to be tested.

The mothers who spoke with me provided a number of explanations
for why they thought the incest happened in their families. The reasons
they gave centered around their sexual estrangement from their husbands; their perceptions of pathology in their husbands; intergenerational
themes; a patriarchal world; and precipitating stresses and turning points.
Finally, the mothers talked about who was ultimately responsible for
the incest.

HUSBAND-WIFE SEXUAL ESTRANGEMENT

Svend Reimer, in an early research note, provided what has proved
to be a classic explanation of father-daughter incest: "With almost no

exceptions, [the father], shortly before the incestuous relationship begins, finds himself barred from sexual intercourse with his own wife."[6] The quality of the husband-wife sexual relationships among the mothers in this study varied. At one common level the mothers described sexual estrangement at one time or another, but for different reasons; and these reasons shed some light on the simplistic "sexual estrangement" theory. Sexual relationship patterns did not remain the same throughout the marriage nor were they defined or experienced in the same way by all the mothers. Ann talked about her own situation and how she felt about it:

> I really felt in so many instances that I wasn't a good wife, and that was the reason for everything he was or wasn't—sexually, for one thing. I believe if a man doesn't have a sexual partner he's satisfied with—this was my reasoning because I think that was a very natural part of his life. He wanted sex pretty often, and I knew I wasn't delivering right.

While only Ann felt that her poor sexual performance as a wife may have contributed to his turning to their daughters, four of the mothers who spoke with me described unsatisfying sexual relationships with their husbands, for which they provided a range of different reasons: religious conflict; alcohol abuse; and the husband's preferred sexual practices.

Ann attributed her inability to be a satisfactory sexual partner to the conflict she experienced between her religion and the use of birth control, and her fear of becoming pregnant:

> I was raised and married in the Catholic Church. I knew we were going to use birth control, and it was a tug with me; I didn't feel too good about it. Maybe I wouldn't have had the conflict if we hadn't been married in my church. Then when I almost died [following the birth of her first child] I thought it was my just desserts for having used birth control. And then when I realized I was going to live, I knew it was a problem. How was I going to relate [sexually] in a marriage? If my husband had been able to come home [from overseas during the war], then we could have talked about it. But he did not come home then. So I decided I was going to offer him a divorce and his child if he wanted her. But I never got to because he came home and surprised me. And his attitude—he was incensed and enraged! He wanted me to be receptive to him.

Ann went on to explain that it was her fear of pregnancy, not any lack of sexual pleasure, that caused her to pull away from her husband:

> After that—it wasn't that I didn't want to sleep with him, but I sure as heck didn't want to get pregnant either. I had limitations, physical, emotional, financial—and I didn't feel I could deal with eleven or twelve children. I probably felt that two was fine, and I had two more than two. When I was pregnant, having sexual relations was fine. There was no fear. I enjoyed sex then.

Another reason for sexual estrangement was alcohol abuse. Four of the fathers had problems with alcohol, but only Bonnie and Cathy related alcohol abuse to the lack of a satisfying sexual relationship. Bonnie described what sex was like with her husband:

> We had no good sex. We rarely had sex, and when we did, it was just a blow job in the morning. I'd do anything to get it over with. He was never once concerned that I had not climaxed. He had a very low sex drive, and it finally just disappeared. The more he drank, the more evident that was. . . . Before I was pregnant with my first son, I did not view sex as unsatisfactory. But afterward, when things got bad, making love was the most demeaning thing to me. I hated that man. He did not meet my needs. He was always drunk. When I wanted to do it, he was drunk and not capable, or not there. He withdrew physically, then I withdrew emotionally.

Cathy reiterated the same theme about her husband when his drinking escalated:

> I didn't like going to bed with him anymore. I always felt as if he was just some old drunk. I never knew if he was even going to stay awake. I felt like he was using me, and I resented that.

Sometimes the husband's preferred sexual practices contributed to the mother's description of an unsatisfying sex life. Ann expressed her feelings about oral sex:

> More and more he wanted oral sex, and I reached a point where I wasn't happy with it, didn't agree with it, and there was a rather abusive incident in relation to that, so that really turned me off.

Bonnie said she did not like oral sex either:

> He liked oral sex. I didn't like it. I just hated it. It was very hard to make him climax, and he wanted to be climaxed orally. It was physically unpleasant because he was such a large man and my jaws hurt. . . . Sex wasn't even fun.

Fay agreed that sex with her husband was no longer any fun for her; it had become a boring routine:

> He asked me, "Well, how come you don't like sex anymore?" I said, "Because it's no fun. It's just—everything is planned. I want to do something different. It's too routine." He was very much of a perfectionist in everything. And sexually, everything had to be just so. I would take a shower, and he would take a bath. I would get undressed and wait for him to get done, and he would get into bed and there was some foreplay, but not much. And we'd have oral sex, or I would mostly have oral sex on him. I used to do it to him, and he would do it to me. I enjoyed it as much as he did, but I would end up doing it more than he would, and I felt like, "Well, to hell with him.

I'm not going to do that anymore if he can't do it to me." Then it got to those kinds of feelings, you know, very inhibited, feelings where I'll give so much, but if I don't receive, if I'm not on the receiving end, well, I'm not giving. But it was mostly routine—this would happen, that would happen, everything the same, and I would say, "I'm getting bored with this. Let's try something else." It was always after the kids went to sleep. It's been a long time since it ever happened during the day or even in the morning. It was all very, very planned, and I felt like I had to have an appointment.

While some of the mothers provided information about sexual estrangement, Cathy discounted it in her own marriage. She talked about her own open and satisfying sexual relationship with her husband:

In the beginning I was very quiet and very shy about sex. There were a lot of things that I didn't know, and he taught me that if you love someone, sex is right, it's just part of life, it's not wrong. He taught me to do lots of things. At first I didn't want to do them, but he'd talk me into it, and I think that's where I got this openness from—it's from him. . . . I used to ask him, "Are you oversexed or what?" Because everybody else said that when you're first married, it's every night, and then it tapers off to two or three times a week in your thirties. We had sex at least every night, and I can't remember not enjoying it.

If there was any withholding on Cathy's part, it was not because she didn't like sex but because she was involved in something else:

Sometimes I used to say, "Look, we just got done two hours ago. Can't you leave me alone?" Especially if I got into doing something. If I was scrubbing a wall or reading, he'd start, and I'd say, "Can't you wait until I'm done here?" It wasn't because I didn't want sex. It was just because I wanted to finish what I'd started, or because I wanted to read longer. And he'd say, "I can't stand it when you're doing something else." So we'd go to bed.

Cathy described herself as multiorgasmic, and I was struck by her almost childlike, unabashed directness as she described her own sexual response pattern:

But I figured if you're going to go to all the bother to get undressed and go to bed just to have sex, you know, in the middle of the afternoon, if I wasn't going to come four or five times, there wasn't sense in doing it. I couldn't believe some of my girlfriends saying it took them a half hour even to get up to that point. In fifteen minutes, I could come five times. And after we would always stay there and cuddle each other. Because at first he would just want to roll over and go to sleep, and I'd say, "I don't want you to do that. I want you to hold me." But he was always used to sleeping by himself and sleeping all over the bed, while I was used to sleeping with a teddy bear. I went from a teddy bear to him, you know.

While Cathy reported a satisfying sexual relationship with her husband, she also described a time when she rejected her husband sexually, although she did not define this as sexual estrangement. Following the birth of their third daughter (within three years of the birth of the first child), she was physically incapacitated with a postpartum complication and was hospitalized off and on over a period of five months. While hospitalized, she left her husband and two older daughters in the care of a neighbor, giving the baby to her mother, who lived near the hospital. Soon after, she learned her husband had become sexually involved with another woman during this time. Cathy told me how she confronted her husband directly and gave him a choice:

> I told him, "I love you, and I want you to come home, but I'm not going to have you come home living with me and running around with everybody else." He decided that he wanted to be at home. For over a year we lived together. He'd never tell me he loved me or anything. He didn't run around, but we just lived together. I'd fix dinner. If he was there to eat it, fine. If he wasn't, that was fine, too. I wouldn't do his laundry. I told him, "Hey, I don't know how you feel or anything. But you can live in this house, and I live in this house because we can't afford anything different, but I'm not taking care of you. I'm not doing anything for you until you are ready to be my husband and treat me right." So that's the way it was for a year. And we didn't have any sex. We just lived in the same house. I told him, "Hey, when you had it, and there was nothing wrong"—it wasn't like I was frigid or anything like that. We had a good sex life, but he wasn't satisfied. "You had to go out," I said. "I'm not going to sleep with you. So you're either going to make up your mind: it's me or other women. And in the meantime, you're not going to be playing around." So he never asked me for sex. He told me he didn't know what he wanted.

Here we have an example of sexual estrangement due to Cathy's temporary incapacity and absence, which resulted in her husband seeking sex with someone else. But Cathy was not a passive, accepting woman. She confronted her husband when she discovered his affair, gave him a choice, and waited until he decided what he wanted, her or the other woman. But, what did he do during that year? To whom did he turn?

Cathy did not feel responsible for her husband seeking sex outside their marriage. She went on to explain why she thought her husband had the affair. It was not because of her absence from the home, but because he was unsure about himself and what he really wanted:

> I don't think I had anything to do with him running around. It wasn't because of a lack of something at home. It was because he was unsure of himself, and that's why it took him so long to decide whether he really loved me and if he was really happy.

There is one last aspect to sexual estrangement that is seldom, if ever, included in the various theories about the etiology of incest. It is generally assumed that the sexual estrangement is initiated by the wife. Ellen described being sexually rejected by her husband:

We were going for marriage counseling. At the time I really didn't think there was anything wrong with our sex life. Sex didn't really matter. I could be happy without it. The counselor asked my husband why he married me in the first place. And he said, because I was a good cook, a good housekeeper, and a good mother. And then he told the counselor he could have just hired a maid instead of getting married. And it suddenly made a lot of sense to me. I knew he didn't love me and that he never would. I thought back to the times he wouldn't return my affection or love. About the times he said, "Don't touch me. I don't know if I love you." If you were married to my ex, you didn't feel like a—how can I put it? You just felt like an object, like a chair, like something he used and phffft, he didn't want anymore. That's the way I felt married to him.

Sexual estrangement as an explanation for incest is probably not considered as valid today since "social workers can find cases which disconfirm the importance of that characteristic."[7] Sexual estrangement in itself, when it is present, is not enough of an explanation, as the mothers above have illustrated. There may be very good reasons for such estrangement, which include variables beyond the culpability of wives.

THE PATHOLOGICAL FATHER

Clinicians have not been able to ascertain that fathers who commit incest are any more pathological than fathers in general. Groth has stated that while there was no distinct characteristics distinguishing incest offenders from other individuals, they did tend to exhibit a number of common characteristics, including "deep-seated, core feelings of help-lessness, vulnerability, and dependence."[8]

While the mothers in this book did not provide enough information about their husbands to make any inferences about their psychological makeup, they all perceived their husbands to be "sick" in one way or another, primarily because they did not see sex between themselves and their children as wrong. And it was to this perceived "sickness" that they turned to explain the incest in their families. Ellen believed her husband was sick because he believed he could get away with it:

My ex is a very sick but brilliant man, and I'm quite sure he knew what he was doing all along. And I'm sure he knew he'd get away with it.

Diane knew her husband's ideas were warped even while he saw nothing wrong with them:

He had made remarks at different times that he thought maybe society was wrong. That these children should be educated like some tribes take the youngsters and do this and that. Therefore, I don't think he thinks it is wrong.

Fay, too, described what she believed to be her husband's sick ideas about right and wrong:

> I think the reason why he did it was because—I feel that he honestly didn't think it was wrong. He's a sick person. I honestly think that it was something he thought he could get away with. That he thought he had his own little harem right there. He knew it was wrong morally because he had been brought up a very strict Christian all his life. You don't smoke, drink, steal. You don't have sex without being married. You don't commit incest. You don't molest children. He knows that but deep down in that sick mind of his he kept telling himself that it's okay.

Another aspect of the mothers' perceptions of their husbands' pathology had to do with their drinking. Three mothers saw a direct relationship between their husbands' drinking patterns and the incest event. Bonnie was inclined to rationalize her husband's behavior because he had a problem with alcohol:

> I think his alcohol pattern is very significant. I do think he might not have been aware of his act. She told me he was drunk when it happened.

Cathy, too, said alcohol made it possible for her husband to do what he did:

> The only thing, the only reason I can even think of to explain his doing that to her is because of the alcohol. Because it would allow him to do things he wouldn't do if he was sober. It would allow him to lose control.

Cathy also believed her husband's drinking was a cause of the incest because it did not continue after her husband dried out following a hospital stay for hepatitis:

> From the time she was fourteen on, nothing happened. He had been in and out of the hospital because of having hepatitis and being alcoholic, and after the first time he was in the hospital he dried out and went home and talked to her and said he realized what had been happening was wrong. They had an understanding that it wouldn't go on anymore, and that if it did, she should go and tell me or go to the police or something like that. He told me he said to her, "I know what I've done is wrong. I feel real bad about it. I don't want it to happen anymore, and I want you to know that if it does, do something about it."

Fay explained her husband's alcohol abuse as a "sickness" within an overall pattern of compulsive behavior:

> It took awhile before I realized my husband's drinking was a sickness and he is a very sick and compulsive man. Soon after our marriage, his sense of humor faded away, and crudeness, meanness, and selfishness took its place. . . . He has no concept of how to control himself over anything. He was very compulsive. If he sees something he wants, no matter what it takes, he'll do it. . . . He was very compulsive about everything. When he was drinking, his whole personality changed.

Alcohol abuse has long been associated with the sexual abuse of children and used by sexual offenders as an excuse of their behavior.[9] The three mothers whose husbands had drinking problems tended to agree; alcohol abuse was part of their husbands' sickness and provided an excuse for them to have sex with their daughters. The alcohol either weakened already weak controls or provided a blackout of their behavior.

INTERGENERATIONAL THEMES

Just as theory has moved from individual to family systems explanations, so did the mothers as they talked. Clinicians and researchers have long viewed incest as a symptom of family dysfunction that is handed down from one generation to the next, with incest victims growing up to become the mothers of incest victims.[10]

Only two of the mothers in this book had been sexually abused by a family member, although not by a father. Diane was molested by an uncle and an older brother but said she chose to push the memory of the experience to the back of her mind:

I was molested as a child, not by my father, but by an uncle and a brother. I talked a little about it to the psychologist, but I didn't say a lot. I guess it's just one of those things I don't want to talk about. I've accepted it in my own way—and I just don't want, you know, to talk about it.[11]

Ellen was sexually abused by two older brothers and she spoke of her own mother's reaction:

I was sexually abused by my brothers—from the time I was five. I don't know if it started earlier or not; that's the earliest I remember. And I made the mistake of telling my mother. I say mistake because my mother was an alcoholic and she flipped out. She called the police and dragged all that in and it was a bad scene in my mind. And it really didn't help, because, when my one brother who got sent away to reform school got back, it started all over again.

In addition to the childhood sexual abuse of Diane and Ellen, the incest occurred across the extended family in three of the families. Ann's husband molested two daughters and a granddaughter; Diane's husband was incestuous with two daughters; and Bonnie's husband sexually abused his stepdaughter and his wife's cousin and there was some suspicion that he had also molested a niece. Yet none of the mothers focused on or attributed much importance to this transgenerational theme or, if they were sexually molested as children, connect their own experience to their daughter's incest.

Associated with incest as an intergenerational phenomenon is the notion that "Incest survivors seem to have an uncanny compulsion to choose partners who are remarkably inadequate and capable of a great deal of physical and sexual violence."[12] While blaming the mother is becoming less popular, the mother's choice of an incestuous partner is still seen by some as an important contributing factor. A recent letter to the editor in response to a report of Margaret Myer's study[13] dismissed the incestuous family myth of the collusive mother and stated:

> Just as it is an inescapable fact that the initiator bears responsibility for the incestuous act itself, it is equally inescapable that the mother (a) chose to associate with a man capable of such an act, and (b) exposed the child to that man.[14]

Bonnie made a connection between the incest and her choice of husband and asked:

> How could it have happened? I'm going back to how could I have picked this man? How did this man come into my house? How did I marry an alcoholic and not know it? Cause and effect is because I married him. I married this man out of sheer naivete; out of low self-esteem. It's also his low self-esteem. His drinking was not a cause, but a release of inhibition. My husband didn't think he was good enough to be with a mature woman, so he went with a child. I don't think it was sex, I think it was power.

Bonnie "knew" a lot about the dynamics of incest and may have been speaking out of an integration of what she knew cognitively and experientially. But she was fumbling for loose threads—weaving together in her own mind her poor choice of spouse out of her own low self-esteem with the sexual abuse of her daughter.

Fay reiterated the same theme but offered a somewhat different explanation for her choice of husband:

> When I look back to my childhood, I was very unhappy. My Dad never sexually abused me, but he physically abused me and my sisters and brothers. He also mentally abused my mother. Now here I am, all grown up, and I find myself in an unhappy situation all over again. I picked a man a lot like my father. They both drank too much and have very bad tempers. What I felt drew me to my husband is that he was always clowning around and he was a lot of fun. My brothers and I used to drink and clown around a lot together. I felt at home with him.

Intergenerational themes were present in one form or another in the families of all the mothers. Certainly the dynamics of family relationships are passed on, whether they are manifested in incest or not. Ann, Bonnie, and Fay, of all the mothers, were the most open and articulate in questioning their own role in the incest. For Ann this was more in the area of her own lack of knowledge, which left her vulnerable to her husband's definition of the situation. But for Bonnie and Fay, it had to do with their husbands to begin with. But beyond the family context lay the patriarchal world.

PATRIARCHAL WORLD

The mothers described a "world of the father," a world that extended from the private domain of the family to the larger, public, societal domain. In this world men had the right to do what they wanted.

Feminist theory sets incest within the context of a patriarchal society and characterizes the incest-family as one where sex-role segregation and the power of the father prevails.[15] I have already discussed the mothers' perceptions of their husbands' abusive power in the family, which some of them related to their inability to prevent the incest from happening or to protect their daughters while it was going on.

But the "world of the father" extended beyond a man's authority over and rights to the females in the family. Socially prescribed patterns of behavior influenced the structure of the family and the positions and roles of males and females within the family system. All the mothers in this study came from traditional families where they learned that women were confined to the home and were expected to take care of the house and children. Men went out into the world and were expected to work and pay the bills.

Bonnie learned clearly defined expectations of a woman's place and role in the family. Bonnie said she fully expected to follow in the footsteps of her mother:

> I was going to be a stereotyped full-time housewife just like my mother. She was my role model. You go to college, you work for a couple of years, you get married, and never work again. Mothers who worked weren't cool. They were either "moochers" [expecting others to do their job] or poor. My mother expected me to get married and to fulfill her role. But she never taught me how to do this and at the same time I was supposed to be smart and get good grades. It wasn't like she kept me out of the kitchen so I could study. But if I got good grades, I wouldn't be popular.

Despite Bonnie's expectations of being a full-time housewife, she described the male-female roles she and her husband played in the family in a somewhat different way: they were not so much egalitarian as they were one-sided:

> My husband was not a chauvinist in the classical sense. There was a mix of sex roles in the family. He cooked, and I painted the house and mowed the lawn, but I resented it because he was drunk and unavailable to do this work, and he got credit for the house looking good. I took over both male and female roles. Male-female roles were not a problem in our family. I felt free to do what I wanted to do, but parent-child roles were definitely screwed up.

Diane also saw and learned how to play her part in a very traditional family scenario:

> I was expected to be there when he left in the morning and at night when

he came home. I was expected to get up and pack his lunch, get his breakfast. And I did it. There were no complaints. My mother had done it for my father, and therefore I really felt that it was part of my duties. I said he supported us and that I should contribute, too.

Three of the mothers learned about expected male-female sex roles from their parents but described a different reality in their own marriages. Cathy said she and her husband had a more egalitarian relationship than her mother and father:

In my family my mother was responsible for the house and children, and my father worked and paid the bills. Normally I don't even think about me being a woman because my husband doesn't say, "Well, you're a woman. You can't do that." He always tells me, "Well, you're really mechanically minded. I knew you could figure that out." And I figure he has certain responsibilities around home, too, not just to go to work and come home and sit in a chair all night. He cooks, and I mow the lawn and help him work on the car. I don't think of it being men's work and women's work.

Fay learned and knew well how the traditional family model worked but said she expected husbands and wives to behave differently in her family:

My husband's always done most of the cooking. Sometimes he'd do the dishes, vacuum, make the bed. But after a while he got lazy and expected me to do it all. I felt [housework] was everyone's work. I never mended his clothes. He was brought up in a very traditional family. Mother did this, mother never went out to work, and father did that. Wives are supposed to submit to their husbands, and looking at my own family, that's how they were too, but I feel that's not the way it should be. He would tell me he didn't think it should be that way either, but then he would act differently.

Sex-role segregation involved more than what women did inside the home; it also involved what they did outside the home. All the mothers except Ann worked outside the home at one time or another, and going to work had a different meaning for the mothers than it did for their husbands. For the mothers it meant getting out of the house, some financial security, and maintaining some control over their lives. For the husbands, it meant a loss of authority and control over their wives, a loss of status, the loss of their wives. Three mothers described the "work issue" in their families.

Cathy said she wanted to work to get out of the house, but to her husband a working wife reflected an inability to fulfill his role as breadwinner:

"No wife of mine is going to go to work." That was the biggie. Probably because that's what he always heard his father say. See, it's the man's responsibility. If you are a man, you are responsible, and you are the breadwinner.

It [his wife's working] meant [to him] that you weren't a man, or you weren't successful, or you failed in some way. I went to work because I wanted to get out of the house. My kids were in school, and I hated housework. But he didn't like it because he felt he didn't have control of me anymore.

Diane explained that both she and her husband believed women were supposed to stay at home:

When we got married, I wasn't allowed to work. I had to quit my job to get married. . . . Everybody thought I went back to work after nineteen years because I wanted to have even more than I had. And I says, "No. I'm quite happy in my home." We had been married nineteen years, and we had built this home. It was free and clear. Everything in it was ours. We didn't owe anybody, and I'm not one who needs a lot.

But she said the time came when she wanted to go to work:

The main reason I want to work is for security. He didn't have any insurance. He didn't have hospitalization or life. There was nothing. And if he left me— he said there was another woman—and I felt if he left me, I wouldn't have nothing. I went to work for security.

Bonnie said she wanted to work to gain some control over her life. At first her husband did not object:

I don't think I had to fight to go to work. He was really from the other side of the tracks, and women going to work was old world to him. His mother and sisters worked. To him, I was not going to work as a new career woman. I was going to work to bring in money. But I went back [to work] to leave myself an out and to maintain some control over my life.

While associations have been made between the incest-family mother's absence from the home because of work and the incest event, David Finkelhor found that "daughters of mothers [who worked] were not at higher risk" of being sexually abused.[16] But Bonnie related her emotional absence to the onset of the incest, and Fay said the incest took place when she was working and physically absent from the home:

I started working because he was on unemployment, and he was home a lot then. He was taking care of the children. It was during summer vacation and he was home alone a lot with her while I was working, and it happened almost every day, she said.

The "world of the father" was real to the mothers in this book. They had been socialized to believe that their husbands had legitimate authority and rights over them in the family and that sex-role segregation in the home was the norm. Yet some of the mothers worked outside the home, even over the objections of their husbands. This meant they found ways to defy or work around their husbands' authority. When they did work outside the home, the balance of power shifted, not only in terms of their access to alternative resources, but also in terms of their husbands' perceived loss of power.

Diane explained the incest within a larger patriarchal world. It was a man's world and within this world men could do certain things and get away with them simply because they did not define them as wrong. Diane talked about the difference in the way men and women viewed incest:

> Some of the men friends that know what has happened, they don't seem to think this was wrong, and you can definitely see they side with him on this. They say, "Oh, that was all right for him to do that." And one of the biggest things I've found is that he is completely accepted in our circle. Nothing has really changed. . . . I get the general impression men seem to think, "So what? It don't matter." Now the women take a very dim view of this. A very dim view. They're horrified. One of my biggest thoughts is—these men, even the ones I would never suspect this of—do they think it's okay? Is it all right for a man to do this to his daughter? Or to another child? Anyone? This is the one thing that I think today still bothers me; that it seems to be accepted. I have found very little support from men.

Diane continued, enumerating the women she knew who had spoken to her about their own sexual abuse:

> After I finally admitted this happened, I did talk to girlfriends and my own family. I couldn't believe the amount of people who said, "I was molested." I took a stand and said, "Here, it's going on." I can't tell you how appalled I have been since I have admitted this. A lot of people, just about everyone I'd come into contact with—I can tell you right now, there's been at least four times as many women tell me they have been molested than say they weren't. For a while I was beginning to think everyone was molested. You just wonder how it can go on for so many people and nobody says nothing. I hope that someday someone somewhere cares enough to make it stop, somehow. I don't think men should be allowed to get away with this.

The "world of the father" encapsulated the mothers, but some of them saw through it and broke out in different ways. As much as I subscribe to the feminist, patriarchal incest-family thesis, after talking to the mothers in this book I began to appreciate the potential of mothers to find ingenious ways to sidestep the power of patriarchy within the family. But any reactive response by mothers to the status quo is a stress to the homeostatic balance of the family system, a stress that in turn requires some kind of adaptive response from the father.

STRESSES AND TURNING POINTS

Some researchers have explained the onset of the incest event as an adaptive behavioral response to stress.[17] Kathleen Tierney and David

Corwin have suggested that in addition to such socio-ecological factors as family structure and individual predisposition, a situational factor such as a significant life stress may lead to "inappropriate acting-out behavior" such as sexual abuse, particularly in the absence of good coping and problem-solving skills.[18]

The mothers who went to work outside the home marked this as a significant turning point, a major transition in their lives. It involved making a decision, standing up to and acting against their husbands' authority. This change in behavior was not an isolated event and often followed or stimulated other ways in which they asserted themselves. In going to work the mothers entered new relationships, took on new roles, and developed new ideas about themselves. Their individual development and growth seemed to represent a new strength that was stressful for their husbands. Bonnie experienced work as a major turning point in her life, and she described it as stressful to her husband. She was growing out of one role into another, and this transition was embedded in and related to other changes:

> I think very much of what I was was what I felt dictated or programmed by society to be as a woman. I was shedding things—that my mother was a housewife all her life and I was doing different things. . . . I stopped being one of the children in the family and grew up. I went back to work first for the money. I was not a career person, and I was really not a professional. But I felt very good about what I could do. I was very competent but had not made it into what I would consider a real professional level. But I became more and more committed and started to rise. That's when the game of him being the father and me being the child ended, and that's when he refused to have it end. It was such a critical time. I mean in the unmasking of the games and roles in that family. I can see the shift when I shut him out.

Bonnie told me what going back to work and being successful meant to her husband:

> He got resentful of my success. In looking back I sometimes think that he tried to kill me, and maybe in me living, I killed him emotionally. I was beaten down. I thought I was worth nothing. And I pulled myself up by going back to work. There's the transition. She tells me it was in kindergarten when this happened. Kindergarten was a major shift in my attitude. The more he pushed me down, the stronger I pushed up. And in him trying to weaken me, I got stronger. I had to believe in myself to get over him communicating that I shouldn't believe in myself.

Working outside the home was a stress and turning point in the families of Bonnie, Cathy, and Diane. But the mothers also experienced and reported numerous physical stresses that included frequent and difficult pregnancies; close, multiple childbirths; postpartum complications; gynecological problems; all of which led to their absence from the home. Ann described the stress in her family around childbirth, which meshed with the other problems that she associated with the onset of the incest:

> My husband was feeling dissatisfaction with the job, and he felt burdened with a large family. I had a rough time after the birth of my second child. I was feeling down, physically. It was after that that he didn't want to use even a condom, and he wasn't too happy about withdrawal, and so this whole thing started up again at that point. Then I had my next two children fairly close. I love children, but I also realized I was maybe having them not for the best reasons in the world. It was to relieve that demand and that pressure [to have sex].

Ann went on to explain how her exhaustion after such frequent childbirths necessitated a rest—away from the family:

> I think it was after my last child that it happened with my oldest daughter. Anyway, the doctor said I needed a rest after she was born, and that I should get away for a week or two just to recoup. She must have been a month old, maybe. I made arrangements and did go spend time with a friend in another state. I was away a little over two weeks; I went by myself. My husband wanted me to go alone. I was going to have my mother come, but at this point she wasn't getting along too well with my husband, so I didn't think that would work so I did not call her to come. We were going to try to get someone, and he said he thought he had a line on somebody that would come in, but as it turned out I think he took time off, and my friends in the neighborhood also helped with the children. But then it evolved that part of the time he stayed home with the children. My oldest daughter associates this time when it [the incest] started.

Emotional stress was present around significant losses through the death of family members, depression, suicide attempts, emotional breakdowns, the frequent hospitalization of a family member, and a husband's drinking and unpredictable behavior. Situational stresses revolved around geographical moves, the husband's dissatisfaction with his job, unemployment, and bankruptcy.

Only Bonnie specifically noted that the incest began around the time of a series of events culminating in a major family upheaval. The whole family changed: Bonnie became pregnant, her mother died, her first son was born, she suffered postpartum depression and contemplated suicide, and then she returned to work.

All families experience stress, but all stress does not lead to incest. But what is significant here is seeing how a mother who begins to grow up, who becomes stronger and assertive within the patriarchal family, may be providing a stress, which along with other factors may trigger the incest response. It is ironic. Mothers have been castigated for not being strong or assertive enough to protect their daughters from incest.

From the reports of the mothers in this book, it almost seems as if their newly discovered assertiveness contributed to the incest as it undermined their husbands and became stressful for them. Could this be another double bind for mothers in the incest-family?

We now turn to whom the mothers held responsible for the incest. While they were not sure about why the incest happened, they were much more certain about who was responsible.

Responsibility

> It's him. He's ultimately responsible. It wasn't my daughter; it wasn't me; it was him, and that's where the solution lies.
> (Bonnie)

The question of who was ultimately responsible for the incest event has found a convenient answer within the family systems explanatory framework, which states that incest is a "three-way process" involving the mother as well as the father and daughter.[19] The mothers who spoke with me attributed responsibility to either themselves or their husbands but identified their husbands as the ones most responsible for the incest.[20] They made no attempt to relieve their husbands of the blame and expressed little concern for any reasons he might have given and little understanding or tolerance for his behavior, even when they may have been empathetic to what the disclosure was doing to him and the family. The father was ultimately responsible for the incest event. Cathy held to this position even when she told me that while her husband took most of the responsibility, he would not assume all of it:

> One of the things he has said to me is he will take ninety-nine percent of the blame, but it wasn't all his fault. He told me it was mutual. Well, I don't buy that for a minute. I just can't accept that. That's meaning she allowed it. And it's not my fault. I didn't change. I still wanted sex as much as I did before.

Ellen said she would not accept the mother-blaming thesis nor carry any guilt for the incest:

> People say blame the mother because she's supposed to protect the kid. How can I blame myself? I don't feel guilty about it. I didn't do it. My ex did it, not me.

Fay and Bonnie also forthrightly stated the responsibility lay with their husbands, not with them, and certainly not with their daughters.

While the others believed and asserted that their husbands were ultimately responsible for the incest, their own sense of guilt and responsibility was still pervasive. One of the reasons the mothers gave for being willing to speak so openly was their own need to understand how this horrendous event had happened in their families and what their own role might have been. All the mothers but Ellen openly expressed some degree of responsiblity, which they related to their inability to prevent the incest from happening. Bonnie spoke of "arming" herself to protect her daughter:

> If I could come up with anything that made me vulnerable for this situation, it was this lack of armament and this trusting sense, never dreaming that he would molest my daughter.

Ann referred to "arming her daughter" as well as herself:

> He said I was to blame for this. If I were a wise and knowledgeable mother, my children would have been armed, and he couldn't have done what he did because they would have been protected because I had armed them. If I'd been armed, I would have been a protection for the children.

Diane said she did not know what she could have done differently, except to have educated her daughter more:

> I feel I made mistakes. But I don't know what they were. I don't know what I should've done different to have kept this from happening. If I were given the chance to do this over again, I don't know what I would do to keep this from happening. I really don't because, in spite of it all, I still don't talk to my daughter about sex or anything like this. I know I could never talk to a nine-year-old about—you can't say to your child, "Your father is a molester. Be careful," even if you think it. Because here you are, trying to bring this child up to love and respect the father, and in the same respect you're saying he's no good, to an extent. I look back, and I know I failed. No, I don't think I'm responsible, but I still feel—I don't know if I could've prevented it. I probably feel more than anything, I should've educated my daughter more to the fact that it could happen. To say I feel responsible, no, I don't think I could have prevented it. I feel, like I said, I could've educated her more.

The mothers carried responsibility with their husbands, but more than their husbands, they still carried guilt for what happened to their daughters. Bonnie was still working through her guilt when she spoke with me:

> I'm no longer dealing with guilt—of course I am—but I did not foster or perpetuate this. I accept that she saw me in that relationship with him, powerless to stop it. I do not feel guilty over that, and that's why she didn't tell me. I was as much a victim as she was. That's where I am mentally and emotionally too.

Ann, of all the mothers, openly expressed the most overwhelming guilt and responsiblity for the incest event:

Thinking about it generates a lot of guilty feelings because I realize I wasn't that wise, that knowledgeable, but not knowing why I wasn't. Why was it? Where was I? Why wasn't I brought into it? I'm not blaming him, but myself. It creates a certain sense of failure as a "being there" person. I'll always wonder and never know how I might have dealt with it if they had told me; what I might have done. I'll always feel hurt and bothered by the fact that I was one of the parties in this home where this was happening.

Contrary to what the literature has reported about mothers blaming their daughters,[21] none of the mothers in this book blamed their daughters or held them responsible for the incest or the family disruption that followed disclosure. As Bonnie said:

I remember saying, "It's not your fault. Don't feel bad about it." I remember saying all those reinforcing things. There was none of this, "You dirty, vile girl," or anything like that.

Cathy told me her daughter had not done anything wrong, so how could she blame her?

I didn't blame her for anything [the incest, telling the police, disrupting the family]. I don't figure that she did anything wrong. All she did was like I did. He did something wrong, and she decided she wasn't going to take the blame for it and said, "I'm just going to let people know what he did." So, I couldn't blame her. It would be just like he wanted me to keep quiet and take the blame for him, and I wouldn't do that. . . . "He was at fault, and even if you went along with it, you're not responsible." That's what I said to her.

It is hard for any mother to escape the "mother blaming" of culture and society. Some of the mothers in this book were able to look at what they might have contributed to the incest event. But when approached by outsiders, they drew their defenses closer to protect themselves from the echo of their own self-imposed judgments.

The mothers did not really understand, nor could they explain, how the incest happened in their families; confusion still reigned. In general, the reasons they gave were not very different from the explanations found in the literature. But the mothers did offer a deeper understanding of some of these explanations from a different perspective. There were reasons for the sexual estrangement that existed between themselves and their husbands. While the mothers blamed their husbnads for the incest, and condemned them as sick for such behavior, as women they were socialized to assume reponsibility for what happened in the family and felt guilty when it did happen. Yet they felt they could have armed themselves and their daughters in some way to ward off the incest.

Family themes handed down from one generation to the next may influence the way a mother is able to handle the reverberations of her own abuse in her daughter. While they lived in families ruled by their husbands, some found the strength to break out of the patriarchal boundaries. Significant turning points in the family created stresses that may have contributed to the incest. Yet few mothers made any direct connections between the things they talked about and the incest event. Among those who did make some connections, Ann related her own "sexual inadequacy," Bonnie her growth and new-found inner strength, and Diane her perception of the patriarchal world to the incest event.

We now conclude with what the incest event meant to the mothers and what they felt the consequences were for themselves and their families, their daughters, and their husbands.

SEVEN

Meanings

It shatters your life, this whole thing.
(Diane)

One of the central questions guiding this study was what the incest meant to the mothers. We have some awareness of the meaning incest holds for the public at large. It is an unspeakable horror, a violation of children, a transgression against family boundaries, a criminal act. The mothers in this book, while they certainly agreed with the above judgments, approached meaning from a somewhat different perspective. They talked about the consequences of the incest, not just for their daughters but for themselves and their families.[1] It was very important for the mothers to find meaning and to make some sense out of what had happened,[2] and this need to understand was one of the reasons they were so willing to talk to me. It was the focus of their quest and purpose, and so it is fitting that we end their stories with their struggle for meaning. As was the case when talking about other aspects of the incest event, the mothers spoke more easily about themselves and their families than about their daughters.

Consequences for the Mother and Family

The incest event did not mean the same and took on different tones for each of the mothers in this book. Those who consciously felt and expressed the most guilt and responsibility focused on that as a touchstone. The incest meant they were not adequate as parents. Ann spoke thoughtfully as she wondered about herself:

> I still feel hurt and bothered by the fact that I was one of the parties in this home where this was happening. Where was I? I'm not blaming him but myself. I feel it creates a certain sense of failure as a "being there" person. Why, why was I the kind of person who could be put in a box of fear like that and shut up? That scares me about myself.

Some of the mothers saw themselves as victims along with their daughters, and victimization meant, more than anything, being punished.

Diane saw her husband "getting away with it" and felt she and her daughter were the ones who had to pay the price:

> It shatters your life, this whole thing. My heart goes out to the woman. In some ways I feel they're the victim. It seemed like my daughters and I were the ones being punished.

Diane went on to explain what being punished meant: having to make new friends and not being able to return to her job.

> Our friends continue to see him, and I have to make a whole new set of friends. There were a few women friends who did not come around before because he was here, and he was quite flirtatious with them and now that he isn't here they do come more. But as far as the family friends, I very rarely see them. . . . The place I worked, he also worked for them indirectly, and I tried to get back to work, but I don't think I ever will because they need him more than they need me. They don't want to make waves. Therefore, I can't get a job now, but he does have one.

Cathy talked about the loss of her husband's income and doing without as a punishment she and her children did not deserve:

> I've really been hurt by all this. I feel that the girls and I are being punished just as much if not more so than he is. Because we don't have the income. The girls are suffering because I have to either go to work or be on welfare. And there is no work. I don't have enough money for us to go to a movie. I can't go out and buy them something just because I want to. We don't have anything now. We're always worried about it. The girls will babysit and say, "Mom, will you take us to the Dairy Queen?" And I'll say, "I don't have the money," and they'll say, "We have the money." And I'll say, "Well, the gas tank is empty and I don't have the money for gas."

Cathy also had to carry responsibility for the family alone, to do things she had not done before, not only during the crisis of disclosure, but after the crisis had passed and her husband had been incarcerated. Cathy told me how hard it had been and still was:

> The hardest thing for me since he's been away is having to do everything by myself. And anything different that I've never done before, it's really hard on me. Right from the time he was arrested, having to go to talk to different people, like the lawyer, having to go to the courtroom, just going to the jail and not knowing how to go about seeing him and things with the rules or the regulations. It was worrying about the bills and how I was going to pay them, how I was going to manage. Just not knowing what's going to happen now. What's going to become of my life. I just felt like my whole life fell apart. I think that was the hardest part.

Cathy, for whom honesty was an important value, also talked about being deeply hurt by her husband's betrayal.

It hurts to know he betrayed me like that. He hurt me. He sneaked around my back and did something to hurt me.

The incest often meant different and sometimes contradictory things to the same mother. The feelings of being punished often gave way to seeing the consequences in a new light. First, Fay spoke of being stabbed in the back and being betrayed:

I've been victimized, stabbed in the back. It's just a hurtful thing to think that I trusted somebody, somebody that you're married to and you love and you think, "I'm going to work. I'm going to help support the family." And here he's doing something like this. I was just overwhelmed with being stabbed in the back. How could somebody who loves you do something like that?

Then Fay reframed the punishment as an opening, a way out, the last straw, and a good reason to end her marriage:

Not all marriages are made in heaven, and I believe this is one that has not been brought together under the Lord's eyes. This is a mistake in my life and this is my way that I must correct it, just divorce my husband and start all over again. . . . His mother's telling me that I should work on mending our marriage back together. After this, I told her there was no way I would even consider ever going back with this person. . . . I know people have gone to counseling and stayed together. If this was the one problem we had, if he didn't have any problems with compulsiveness or drinking or gambling, it might be worth mending your family back together. But I consider him a real sick person. He's a compulsive drinker, gambler, he stole, he went bankrupt.

Fay also saw the disclosure of the incest as an opportunity for a new kind of relationship with her daughter:

It woke me up. It opened my eyes where I could understand a little bit the way I reacted toward my daughter. It's affected our relationship better because it's helping to build a better relationship with her. I've always showed my love materially—a new coat, a dress, an ice cream, but that's not the right way to show your love. I would like to learn to show my love emotionally. I've learned over this problem with her. I can now put my arm around her and tell her, "I love you. We're going to get through this together." But I'm still a little reserved. Maybe I always will be. It's my personality probably, but I can at least show her a little more.

Like Fay, Ellen first focused on her hurt and anger against her husband:

I felt betrayed and hurt and then angry. Not so much with my daughter as I did about my ex. I thought back to the times he wouldn't return my affection or love. About the times he'd say, "Don't touch me. I don't know if I love you."

Then Ellen turned punishment into relief. She may have felt betrayed, but she also felt vindicated for a bad marriage and her poor relationship with her daughter:

All my hurt and bitterness, I think, got out that day I found out. And it was really a relief, not because of what happened to her, but because I stopped blaming myself for my marriage. Wow! This wasn't my fault, not my marriage, not my relationship with my daughter.

As we can see, the coins of consequences for the mothers sometimes had two sides: punishment and betrayal on one side; relief, vindication, a way out, and new opportunities on the other. Crisis can be an opportunity for new growth and opportunities, and for some of the mothers this was true in terms of them individually. But when talking about their families, the consequences of the incest violated their illusions of family life.

Family meant different things to the mothers, and the metaphors they used to express their ideal beliefs and values about family life were quite different from the ways they saw their families after the carnage of incest. Most of the mothers held on to a family fairy tale of closeness, togetherness, and warm, open, affectionate feelings. Diane's notion of family was more concrete: a home, a house. Ellen was the most cynical about family life, "never having had a family" herself. Even while her own family or origin was one of violence, abuse, and alcoholism, she dreamed of family togetherness as it was portrayed in the TV families of the 1950s. But she knew, "Fairy tales don't come true, they can't happen to you."

The family metaphors after the disclosure of the incest were of "empty shells." Ann saw her family as a tree and talked about its branches. When one became infected, the disease spread to all the other branches:

You discover one branch of the family business is in trouble but you do not know the seriousness of it. You think it is going to be all right. After the business has grown and matured and you think you have done the best for it, with some exceptions, then you find out all the other branches are broken, too.

Diane blamed herself for the family disruption that resulted from her actions to protect her daughter:

I had to put my husband out, and the feelings are very deep by how much you hurt him, yourself, and your children. It broke up our home—shattered our lives. . . . One of the hardest things I do think is to break your family up. And that's what you're doing when you put your husband out, regardless of what people think. I said even my own daughter suffered from it, having her father removed from the home, not to mention the other children in the family. The presence of a masculine force to help bring the children up in the right way has been missing.

Daughters are said to be reluctant to tell anyone about the incest event because they feared breaking up the family. Diane expressed the same fear:

> I wanted to keep the house together. I thought this [the incest] would tear it apart, which it did.

As the mothers talked about their families, I sometimes felt that their families were the outer shells of their own identities, that their own sense of themselves and family were one and the same. Just as they felt punished and betrayed, so they saw their ideal images of family destroyed. Incest was the ultimate shock that forced them to face the ultimate disillusionment.

Consequences for the Daughter

As always, the mothers had difficulty talking about their daughters. I believe this was a defensive avoidance that preserved a wall providing some kind of protection against a deeper pain. At first Ann said she could not even think about, much less talk about, what her husband did to her daughter:

> I find it very difficult to talk about—some of the things my daughters shared with me are so—I cannot conceive of someone who—.

But after a while she told me how the incest had hurt her youngest daughter.

> It robbed my youngest daughter of her growing up and discovering her sexuality and robbed her of her late childhood and early teens. It's something that's influenced every other area of her life; her feelings about herself, her self-confidence.

Ann did not minimize the harm done to her daughters and granddaughter. But she told me about the doctor who had:

> Both my daughters have been equally hurt in different areas. My oldest daughter was hospitalized for a drug overdose when she was a teenager. She told her doctor about the incest, but he dismissed it. I think my granddaughter, probably because she has a learning disability, the effect on her for that reason, it is even tougher. My youngest daughter is working it out, but she's spending a lot of her life doing it.

Bonnie, too, encountered professionals who discounted the impact of the incest on her daughter. She recalled an emotional crisis in her daughter's life after her daughter told her about the incest.

> I felt I was living on a time bomb and that it was related to the incest. I was later told by her and the counselor at Crisis Intervention that it was all boyfriend related. I wanted her to go back to Crisis but she said she was fine; she didn't want to go; it was stupid. But I made her go for me. I brought up that my daughter didn't want to talk about it, she didn't think it was relevant, but that she had been molested—and everyone I talked to said it wasn't relevant. Well, I think it is relevant. I think for me it was relevant. I burst out crying. I finally said to her, "Do you know the guilt I feel over what he did to you?" And that was as far as it went. . . . They say there's a life before and after incest, and everything in her life does not radiate from that one event.

In contrast to Ann and Bonnie, Cathy and Diane tended to minimize the impact of the incest on their daughters. Cathy had been concerned about how the incest might have hurt her daughter. But she was very present oriented and pointed to how her daughter was functioning at the time she talked with me as evidence of how well her daughter was actually doing:

> I don't think my daughter's been hurt emotionally. At first I was worried about that. I was worried about how it would affect her sexual life, being married, having kids, things like that. But the way she feels, the relationship she has with her boyfriend, I don't think it's hurt her, scarred her mentally or anything like that. I think it's something that she's learned to live with and not live with any kind of guilt because of it.

Diane talked about the way her older daughter handled the incest, which may have echoed the way Diane coped with her own sexual abuse. If it hadn't affected them, it wouldn't affect her younger daughter; she'd be able to handle it as they had:

> I talked to my older daughter [who was also sexually abused by the father] when this happened [to her sister], and she says, "Well, it didn't hurt too bad." And she says she got over this. It don't affect her. . . . And this daughter, she can handle it now. I really shouldn't have to worry about her.

In contrast, Fay and Ellen were concerned about how the incest would affect their daughters' sense of trust. Fay seemed almost to be talking about herself as she talked about her daughter:

> It's going to be hard for her to trust anybody for a long time. I can feel that. It's so hard for her to trust, you know.

Ellen went beyond trusting anyone now and worried about the time when her daughter would have a little girl of her own:

We talked about how this is going to affect her. I said to her, "If you ever have a little girl, that's going to go through your mind. Especially if the father wants to take the little girl for a walk. Or suppose you want to run next door to see a girlfriend, and while you're gone, it might go through your head all the time what happened to you, and [you'll wonder] what's happening to your little kid."

The mothers really did not want to think or talk about the ways their daughters might have been damaged physically or psychologically by the incest. They had already expressed how painful it was to think about the incest itself. It was almost as if the pain numbed them and served as a blanket to protect them from knowing any further details. And yet each faced reality to her own level of tolerance and spoke in her own way about how the incest may have affected her daughter. Ann, who was the most overwhelmed by the horror of incest, was the furthest away from the incest event in time. Her daughters were in their late twenties and early thirties and the wounds of the incest had had time to fester through the scar tissue. The other daughters were younger, from age 11 to 15. The incest wound was still fresh and the protective scab was protecting the wounds of both the daughters and their mothers.

Consequences for the Father

The mothers did not talk too much about the meaning of the incest for their husbands. If they felt that they were victimized, punished, and betrayed by the incest, and that their families had been shattered and broken, they felt that their husbands "got away with it," which three of them did. Bonnie learned of the incest long after her divorce. Her own fear of her ex-husband restrained her from even thinking about confronting him with her knowledge, particularly since he no longer had any contact with her daughter. Ellen's husband was charged but, because of a legal technicality, the charges were dropped. Diane's husband was charged with incest but denied vehemently that he did anything, and her daughter refused to testify against her father in court.

Three fathers were caught and held accountable. Ann's husband was in a group treatment program for sexual offenders for six months as a condition of probation following disclosure of the incest with his granddaughter. Cathy's husband was serving a prison sentence, and Fay's husband was found guilty and sentenced to a prison term. All three of these fathers admitted to the incest offense, and the consequences for them were very tangible.

Diane and Cathy, the two mothers who planned to reconcile with their husbands, talked about what they felt the disclosure of incest meant to their husbands in terms of the consequences beyond punishment. Diane felt she had hurt her husband terribly by having to evict him from the home in order to protect her daughter; but she said she was satisfied that that might serve as deterrent to a repetition of his behavior:

> I kind of hate to have my husband's name on a record or blotter. But it must be God's will, and maybe this will help him from doing something like this again, knowing it is there.

Cathy explained that her husband's prison sentence forced him to stop and get help for his drinking, which she believed was a cause of the incest:

> In a way, all this coming out in the light has had a kind of positive side. It's the best thing that's happened because it forced him to get the help that he wasn't willing to get before. . . . And he's glad he's had to quit drinking. He's sorry that this had to happen in order for him to quit drinking.

Cathy told me she was determined, however, to reinforce her husband's sobriety:

> The girls are still a little fearful of his coming home because they're afraid he may start drinking again. I believe that he won't drink because I have told him, "If you drink, you know what's going to happen." First of all, if he takes a drink, I'll turn him in. I'll call the police. He'll be on parole, and he won't be allowed to drink. I'd turn him in, yes I would. Because I feel like alcohol is what caused all of this and if the bottle means that much to him, having a drink means so much to him that he'll risk everything, then I've gone through all this for nothing. And he knows that. Because I've really been hurt by all of this, and I'm willing to forgive the hurt. I'm willing to try to live with that if I know he wants to stop the hurt. If he doesn't want to stop it, then I'm not going to go through it. I'm not going to bang my head against a brick wall.

The other mothers had left their husbands or put them out of their lives, and they were not concerned with what the incest might mean to them. At least they did not talk about it. But the incest event was deeply meaningful to the mothers in terms of how they perceived it affected them, their families, and their daughters. Since there is virtually no information about the perceptions and feelings of mothers, any exploration, even a limited one such as this, does provide new insight into and understanding about how incest-family mothers give meaning to the incest event.

A Final Note

Diane and Ann offer us a final note, which provides an appropriate ending to the voices and stories of all the mothers in this book. Diane said:

> I think back, and I wonder why we're all so afraid to tell. I never told my

mother; my daughter never told me 'til I took a stand and admitted it. I just wish it would stop. I hope that this can help somebody else and that somebody somewhere cares enough to make it stop. I don't think men should be allowed to get away with this. The more you hide it, the more it's going to go on. Maybe if our forefathers somewhere had taken a stand against this, maybe it might not be in the epidemic proportions now. Until men realize, "Hey, I can't get away with this," it's not going to stop.

And Ann forecast:

This generation is turning it around. This generation is saying, "NO."

EIGHT

███████

Some Conclusions

Lived events are ambiguous because no
experience comes alone, and so a single
event entails many others.
—John Berger, "The Credible Word"

At the beginning of this book I said I did not want to simply collect and
report facts about mothers of incest victims, but that I wanted to imagine
the experiences that lay behind the events in their lives. Statements
based on theoretical constructs about collusive, powerless, or protective
incest-family mothers simply do not allow us to see the ambiguities
behind these abstractions. The lives of the mothers in this book are
ambiguous, and one way to understand their experiences is to see them
as connected events that take place within a social and cultural context.

I have utilized three perspectives in both listening to and analyzing
the mothers' stories. A sociological perspective has helped me to understand the ways in which their lives have been shaped and influenced by
the gender group to which they belong. The feminist perspective has
directed me to consider the ways their self-reported lives and behaviors
are related to the larger social structures of society.[1] This perspective
has also sensitized me to understand the relationship between the wife/
mother sex-role socialization of women to the structure of male-female
power relationships both within the family and society at large.[2] A third
perspective, the symbolic interactionist, has provided me with an understanding of human behavior as responsive to the meanings people give
to the events in their lives, the behavior of others, and their social
milieu.[3] This perspective is congruent with the feminist "angle of
vision,"[4] which accepts and makes visible the way women describe,
experience, and give meaning to their existence. It also assumes that the
responses and behaviors of people are influenced by their definition of
the situation and the meanings they attach to the behavior of others and
the events in their lives.

It is tempting to defend the mothers I got to know so well against
the prevailing stereotypes about them. And I find myself feeling a certain
ambivalence between what I have come to understand about their lives
from their perspective and a responsibility to acknowledge that all parents, as adults, must be held accountable for what happens to their

children when they are innocent children. This does not mean that I am ignoring the circumstances—some universal, some idiosyncratic—associated with the mothers in this book. Nor am I minimizing what a woman learns about becoming a mother from both her own mother and the society and culture within which she lives.

Most of us who are mothers carry our own brand of guilt and responsibility over what happens to our children. This is the great truth that has been handed down to us, and one that we believe. We do feel responsible and guilty despite the personas we wear to protect ourselves from the criticism we feel from the world at large. So I find myself moving back and forth from the stories the mothers told me to the explanations offered by the theoretical perspectives I have chosen; from my own personal history as the once-angry daughter of a still-living mother, and the still-guilty mother of two adult daughters, to the insights I have gained as a social worker working with mothers with many different kinds of problems with their children.

There are no simple conclusions to the complex stories of the mothers in this book; rather, a patterned tapestry of themes woven from their combined experiences is created. One way to look at these themes would be to hold them up against the collusive, powerless, and protective mother models set forth in the introduction to see how they fit or do not fit the different ideas and beliefs many people still hold today about mothers in incest-families.

The Collusive Mother

As the mothers told their stories they wove patterns that match some of the themes of the collusive mother model. They were absent or incapacitated in some way; they were sexually estranged from their husbands. But underneath these surface statements lay different webs of circumstances that resulted in unique explanations for such behaviors. But the mothers' experiences in other realms of the collusive mother prototype did not match, as they presented variations on the mother-daughter relationship theme around the issue of role reversal, belief, and blame.

ABSENCE/INCAPACITY AND DENIAL

A mother's absence or incapacity has long been associated with her collusion, and there is some evidence that a female child *is* more at risk of incest if her mother is absent or incapacitated in some way. She is vulnerable if she lives apart from her natural mother; if the mother is employed outside the home; or if the mother is disabled or ill.[5] But underlying this evidence of risk is still the tenaciously held belief that mothers are expected to be physically at home and psychologically present; to be sensitive to and to provide for the total needs of all family members. These institutionalized norms about traditional families and the roles of women in the family are as accepted today, even as the roles of women are changing and they are moving in greater numbers from the home to the work world, as they were in the recent past when mothers were more likely to be at home full time.

The literature has given little consideration to the reasons for a mother's absence or her incapacity to fulfill her role as traditionally defined by society. In many families, non-incest as well as incest, mothers are often overburdened with child care and other domestic responsibilities, personal illness, and family stresses of all kinds, with little or no assistance or relief. And when any mother is physically and emotionally overwhelmed, she may tend to be psychologically absent and inattentive. We suspect that mothers of incest victims do suffer unusually high rates of depression,[6] which may account for what has been seen and described as their emotional withdrawal, disinterest, and passivity.

Another dimension of a mother's psychological absence and depression is the issue of her denial of the incest event, for if a mother is not there, she cannot be expected to know. Yet the ever-present question asked about the incest-family mother is, "How could she not know?" And the debate still lingers on whether she knew about the incest or not.[7] Ruth and Henry Kempe are an example of those who take an absolutist position on this issue:

> Stories from mothers that they cannot be more surprised can generally be discounted—we have simply not seen an innocent mother in long-standing incest, although the mother escapes the punishment her husband is likely to suffer.[8]

This belief that mothers do know is refuted by numerous examples in the literature of mothers who did not know.[9] Gilgun, for one, concluded from her research, "Evidence was found that the sexual abuse of one family member by another can take place for several years and no one but the perpetrator and his victim know about it."[10]

There also seems to be some confusion about a mother's ability to distinguish between her responsibility for knowing that the incest was going on and for letting it continue. This is a distinction the literature seldom makes, and it would seem important to differentiate among mothers who (1) actively and directly foster or contribute to the incest; (2) condone or allow the incest to continue while knowing about it; (3) suspect, but are not able to follow up on their suspicions; (4) know, and are unable to confront the offender or try to stop it but fail; and (5) really do not know about the incest event. I believe it is important that we make distinctions among these different levels of "knowing." I also believe we must accept that some mothers simply do not know about the incest while it is going on.

Rooted in the belief that "mothers know" is the assumption that caring, vigilant mothers will be aware of everything that happens to their children, which sets mothers up to be all seeing, all knowing, and to carry total responsibility for what goes on in the family. The role of the unconscious and the defense mechanisms of denial have been used to explain the mothers' protestations of ignorance of the incest, and I do not mean to discount these powerful explanatory theories. But if a mother is overwhelmed with stress or suffering from depression, she may not have the capacity to see and know about everything that is going on in the family.

I do not intend to minimize the risk a mother's absence or incapacity presents for a child in the family, particularly when the father figure may be a potential incest offender. I simply want to emphasize that the maternal absence/incapacity factor may be beyond a mother's control and cannot necessarily be construed as her *active* contribution to the incest event.

The mothers in this book were all physically or psychologically absent or incapacitated around the time the incest began in their families. However, this absence or incapacity cannot be viewed simply as an active abandonment or a turning away from the family or the needs of their daughters. It was related much more to a number of reality factors. Ann's multiple pregnancies and her forced absence from the family during her confinement in a psychiatric institution; the chronic depression Diane suffered in response to the loss of so many family members over an extended period of time; Ellen's way of coping with family chaos; Cathy's withdrawal from her husband in response to discovering his infidelity; Bonnie's and Fay's need to work outside the home to earn needed money for the family; and all of the mothers' responses to physical and psychological abuse. Mothers respond in similar ways to such situations in families where incest does not occur, and these cannot, alone, be considered factors in what has been labeled the incest-family mother's collusion.

The mother's physical or psychological absence can be used to explain the avoidance and denial of the incest while it is going on. "If I am not there, I cannot see or know." It is noteworthy that only Diane and Ellen, the two mothers who had been incest victims themselves as children, suspected the incest.[11] The other four mothers claimed no knowledge about the incest while it was going on, although Bonnie and Fay could look back and see the signs that they felt should have alerted them.

No clear link has yet been established between a mother's own history of sexual abuse and her awareness of the incest, her ability to protect her daughter from incest, or her capacity to be empathetic to her daughter following disclosure. A common assumption is that the mother who herself had been an incest victim should be even more alert to the possibility of incest and want to protect her daughter from a repetition of her own traumatic experience. My own hunch, based on my clinical work with both adult survivors of incest and mothers of incest victims, is that a mother's denial and suppression of her own experience may play into the denial of what may be happening to her daughter. She may believe, out of a defensive denial of her own sexual abuse, that because she survived her incest experience (and usually without any help), her daughter should be able to do the same thing.[12]

In contrast to reports about mothers who say they do not see and do not know and, therefore, do nothing, I am hearing from clinicians in the field about the mothers they are seeing who *are* aware of the incest, or the potential for incest, and have gone to extraordinary measures to protect their daughters in situations where there are few if any services available or accessible to help them. "Many mothers *do* believe their daughters, *do* protect them, *do* act in their best interests, and have always done so."[13]

A mother's awareness or denial of the incest has to be seen within a social context, for to know is to have the responsibility to act, and to act means knowing what to do and how to do it. Just as abused women began to leave battering spouses as more social and legal resources became available, more incest-family mothers may see and consciously acknowledge that the incest is going on as they gain more knowledge about the behavioral signs of incest and as they perceive community social and legal services to be more sensitively responsive to their needs.

SEXUAL ESTRANGEMENT

The mother's sexual rejection of her husband has been advanced as one of the most significant characteristics of the collusive incest-family mother. Male clinicians gave birth to the sexual estrangement theory, and its credence has been subsequently emphasized as a prime variable until a feminist perspective began to focus on the patriarchal nature of the incest-family where all females in the family are potential sex objects "to be used as sexual conveniences."[14]

The assumption underlying the sexual estrangement theory is that a woman becomes the sexual property of her husband upon marriage and is therefore expected to meet and fulfill all his sexual needs, regardless of her own physical or emotional state. And if a wife turns away from her husband sexually, she has collusively contributed to his sin of incest. Another consequence of sexual withdrawal is marital rape. Many women have suffered "legal rape" within marriages where their husbands claim the right to sexually abuse them and where they had no legal recourse to seek protection until most recently with the enactment of marital rape laws in some states.[15]

All the mothers in this book were sexually estranged from their husbands at some time during their marriages. However, this alone provides little understanding about their sex lives. For that we have to listen to the reasons they offered for their sexual dissatisfaction and sexual withdrawal: religious conflict over birth control; fear of continuous pregnancies; their husbands' sexual practices, which they defined as distasteful or boring; sexual rejection by the husband; or sexual withdrawal in response to a husband's infidelity. Ann was the only mother who questioned her own sexual inadequacy as a possible factor in her husband's need to turn to his daughters for sexual satisfaction. Cathy, on the other hand, could not understand why her husband would need to turn to his daughter when their sex life was so mutually rich and satisfying. If we were to look at marital sexual relationships from the perspective of wives in non-incest families, we would probably find that the sexual estrangement theory does not sufficiently differentiate incest-families from non-incest-families since it is estimated that some form of sexual dysfunction is present in most marriages at some time or another;[16] marriages where incest is not the consequence.

While the sexual inadequacy of the mother has been highlighted as a major contributing factor in the family dynamics leading to incest, it is becoming more and more difficult to continue to accept this as a collusive characteristic of mothers any more than we can use it to explain other kinds of sexual excesses or deficiencies on the part of men. If husbands are unfulfilled sexually by their wives, whatever the circumstances, the focus should be on understanding why a man would turn to a child rather than another adult, not on his wife's sexual inadequacy and unresponsiveness.[17]

THE MOTHER-DAUGHTER RELATIONSHIP

At the very heart of the collusive mother paradigm lies the mother-daughter relationship. But before we can look at this relationship through the collusive mother lens to understand how it may impact on the mother's failure to protect her daughter, we first have to look at the institution of motherhood.

Adrienne Rich has described the institution of motherhood as the "keystone" in establishing not only the expected patterns of motherhood—be a good female; be a proper woman; marry, and bear children—but the myth of the perfect mother as well.[18] This myth creates and promotes an ideal mother who is a font of continual, unconditional love; a mother who is everything to her children.[19] And yet, this idealization of motherhood goes against the experience of most mothers, for we know we cannot meet these institutionalized expectations and we blame ourselves for not only having failed our children but for their imperfections as well. This is an old, mother-daughter script that gets handed down from one generation to the next.

The mothers in this book did not voluntarily talk very much about their daughters or their relationships with them. Some hardly mentioned their daughters at all until I specifically questioned them. Their attention was focused much more on themselves and their relationships with their husbands. And when they did mention their daughters, they did not talk about the alienation and conflict themes that have commonly characterized mother-daughter relationships in both incest- and non-incest-families.[20] Only Ellen spoke openly of her alienation from her daughter, and for this she blamed her husband.[21] For the most part, the mothers were unable to think, and much less talk, about what had happened to their daughters, and in their sense of fusion (whether manifested in extreme closeness or distance), some of the mothers felt and expressed their daughter's pain as their own.[22] In fact, they were much more loving and caring for their daughters, albeit bound up with responsibility and guilt, than angry and rejecting. It is important to remember that mothers and daughters in all families will usually have different perceptions of their relationships with each other. We already have information about how incest-daughters feel about their mothers, but we need more information about how incest-family mothers feel about their daughters before we can make any conclusive statements about the dynamics of that relationship and whether or not it is uniquely different from mother-daughter relationships in families where incest does not take place. The contributions, however slim, from the mothers in this book have made a start in that direction.

The mother's role reversal with her daughter, along with sexual estrangement, has been set forth as a significant characteristic of the collusive incest-family mother.[23] While the collusive mother has been indicted for resigning from her assigned female roles of wife and mother and handing them over to her daughter, the social and cultural contexts of female sex roles and mother-daughter relationships provide a richer soil for understanding what has been labeled mother-daughter role reversal. Historically and culturally mothers have been assigned almost total responsibility for children. Mothers are expected to care for and nurture everyone in the family. But when she is overburdened or ill and cannot fulfill her roles and functions, it is not her husband who is expected to help, because his instrumental roles lie outside such female duties: the natural, most available helper is another female in the family, usually the mother's oldest daughter. As the mothers talked I listened for evidence of role reversal, but they did not perceive or describe a reversal of roles between themselves and their daughters. What they did present, though, were different manifestations of role confusion.[24]

In all families generational boundaries separate the parent and child subsystems and mark the positions of family members. The particular status position a family member occupies will define the roles or the behaviors and responsibilities expected of him or her while occupying that position. The mothers in this book described families where parent-child boundary structures appeared at times to be distorted, blurred, and sometimes even erased. They placed themselves, their husbands, and their daughters in family positions that resulted in role confusion and redefined each person's responsibilities, behaviors, and privileges in the family.

I found three major parent-child boundary patterns that deviated from the more functional pattern where both parents are on the adult side of the generational boundary and the children are on the child side. In the first pattern the mother defined herself as a child-wife[25] and placed herself and her daughter on the child side and her husband on the parent side of the generational boundary. In the second pattern, the mother again perceived herself as a child-wife in the marriage, but this time she placed her daughter and husband in the roles of adults on the parent side of the generational boundary. In the third pattern the mother perceived herself as a mother-wife and both her daughter and husband as children, with herself as mother to them both.

Thus, a mother's definition of the role relationships in the family might influence her perception and interpretation of different behaviors as well as what behaviors she might expect and accept as normal. Child-wives do not have authority over parent-husbands or the right to intervene in what they do, whether the mother sees her daughter as a peer or as an adult. Likewise, mother-wives may tend to redefine what child-husbands can do with a child whom she views as his sibling.[26]

In addition to the distortion of the parent-child generational boundary that resulted in role confusion, some mothers attempted to erase the parent-child generational boundary altogether because they viewed such boundaries as potential obstacles to close relationships and a sense of belonging; boundaries symbolized barriers that would keep family members apart. Such boundaries were seen as contributing to possible separation, rejection, loss, or abandonment, strong themes found in incest-families.[27]

Any attempt to make a connection between the mothers' construction of family relationships and the incest event is not warranted at this time. The images and configurations I present here are present in families where incest does not occur; we cannot yet be sure that the dynamics of incest-families are peculiarly different from families in general. The large research projects from which representative samples have been drawn are examining the interactional effects of a wide range of personal and social variables.[28] More knowledge about the incest-family and the dynamics among family members must await the results of these studies before any vaild associations can be made between any unique role relationship patterns of the incest-family and the incest event.

BELIEF AND BLAME

The last prevailing pattern in the collusive mother tapestry is that of belief and blame. Certain clinical reports state that mothers either disbelieved their daughters' reports of the incest or, if they did believe the incest occurred, blamed their daughters. MacLeod and Saraga challenge this "mother-blaming" thesis and provide another context for understanding what may appear to be blaming behaviors, the concept of loss:

> Some mothers do refuse to believe that sexual abuse has occurred, or know and do nothing, or are angry with and blame their daughter, or feel that they are themselves to blame. This is taken as evidence of collusion. Yet we know that denial, anger and guilt are common responses to loss. This kind of event, especially if it occurs within the family, is a tragic loss for everyone. The woman has lost her view of herself as "wife" and mother. She has lost the fantasy family; her family and her relationships with other family members will never be the same again. The desperate desire of many mothers is: "let it not have happened, let it not be true."[29]

The mothers in this book did suffer the losses above but also believed the incest happened regardless of how they found out. There were, however, different stages to their response patterns, ranging from initial shock, disbelief, and denial to belief and acceptance. And it may be any one of these stages in the disbelief-acceptance cycle that clinicians and researchers have misinterpreted as the mother's disbelief in the past. In no instance did a mother in this book blame her daughter. They were quite clear about who was responsible, first their husbands and then themselves.

The Powerless Mother

The question, "Why didn't the mother know the incest was going on?" frames the collusive mother profile. The question, "Why didn't she do something about it when she found out?" frames the picture of the powerless mother. Some have excused the collusive mother by attributing her inability to act to protect her daughter, both before and after the incest event, to her position of powerlessness in the family. And many incest-family mothers do perceive themselves as powerless to change their own or their children's situations.

The mothers who spoke with me did not see or present themselves as passive, helpless, submissive women, and certainly not in all areas of their lives. Nor did they portray their husbands in the one-dimensional, tyrannical terms found in the literature. However, the mothers did tell me about their perceptions and ideas on two dimensions of the powerless mother model: sexual hierarchies within marital power relations and sex-role segregation.

SEXUAL HIERARCHIES AND POWER RELATIONS

Some authorities agree that incest is more an issue of power than of sex. Suzanne Sgroi represents this position:

> Inevitably, the offender's power position in relation to the child victim and

the child's perception of his or her subordinate role are the principle deter-
minants of what happens between them. . . . [30]

And Judith Herman carries the issue of power even further with her
patriarchal family incest hypothesis,[31] yet to be empirically tested, which
suggests that families where incest occurs are more sexually hierarchical
and father dominated than families where incest does not occur.

Three major assumptions underlie the ideas about sexual hierarchies
and husband-wife power relations. The first assumption is that the marital power structure is affected by the ideology that men legitimately
occupy status positions superior to women and therefore have the authority to dominate and control them.[32] The second assumption is that
women have unequal access to economic and social resources with the
result that husbands have advantages over wives in marital exchanges.[33]
The third assumption is that women have been socialized and conditioned to be submissive, passive, helpless, and powerless. However, these
traits alone do not explain why women are relatively powerless or dominated by their spouses. It is unlikely that these traits would differentiate
incest-family mothers from non-incest-family mothers any more than
such traits differentiate battered wives from non-battered wives.[34]

While the boundaries between the generations were distorted and
blurred in the families of the mothers in this book, the boundaries
between the husband and wife were much more clearly delineated, even
for those mothers who may have been "mother-wives." Each position
was firmly marked by the husband and acknowledged by the wife,
although she did not always stay in her place. Yet, all of the mothers
defined their husbands as head of the family in one way or another.[35]
They recognized and believed that their husbands had more authority
than they did, and that their husbands had abused this authority over
their daughters. The mothers were angry about this but accepted it and
were resigned to the reality that it was a man's world and that men
could do and get away with things that women knew were wrong. This
was, in fact, one of the strongest explanations they gave for why the
incest happened: because their husbands did not believe that what they
did was wrong, and that it would continue to be a social issue as long
as men got away with it.

All the mothers experienced some form of psychological and/or physical abuse at some time during their marriages before the disclosure of
the incest event, and all but Cathy were realistically afraid of their
husbands. In this sense the incest occurred within the context of family
violence.[36] However, the mothers' responses to their husbands' use of
power and authority were not similar. Some mothers were assertive;
others were more intimidated by their husbands, particularly if they had
suffered severe psychological or physical abuse. The assertive mothers
spoke back and fought back; the intimidated mothers found other ways

to survive.[37] I believe we need to examine further the husband-wife power relationships in incest-families before we can have confidence in a simple powerless mother or patriarchal family incest hypothesis. Power relations are more intercursive than purely asymmetrical[38] and the bases, process, and outcomes of power relations in families where incest takes place are important collateral issues that need to be considered.[39] I am not saying incest is not a power issue: I believe it is.[40] And regardless of the ways in which the fathers exerted their power in the family, and irrespective of how the mothers negotiated that power, the mothers all felt the incest had victimized them as well as their daughters. But the issue of power in any family must be viewed and understood in light of the way "gender relations [are] sanctioned by the larger society."[41]

SEX-ROLE SEGREGATION

It is difficult to separate, even conceptually, sex-role segregation from sex-role socialization, for both men and women have been socialized to occupy gender-split worlds. The domestic sphere of women is separated from the public sphere of men. The "traditional marital enterprise"[42] divides women's work as homemakers from men's work as wage earners. And along with the traditional division of labor goes a division of authority, a system of patriarchy, and the rule of the father.

The degree of segregation of male and female roles is one of the ways of measuring a patriarchal, father-dominated family. All the mothers in this book learned to be wives and mothers in their own traditional families of origin and they accepted the norms leading to a segregation of sex roles and a separation of male and female domains: men work outside the home and women work inside the home. But strict sexual segregation of male-female roles was not the norm in their families of procreation, and all the mothers in this book, except Ann, worked outside the home, even in those situations where their husbands objected.

Sex-role segregation alone, as a measure of patriarchal, father-dominated family, may not be enough. It can be argued that where the sexual division of labor in incest-families is less rigid, it is because the father agreed to allow it for his own reasons and not because he abdicated any of his patriarchally based authority. Gender definitions of roles within the family evolve from the institutionally entrenched and enforced division of labor in society,[43] but sex roles are changing in the most traditional of families today and may not be valid measures of family power relations in either incest- or non-incest-families.

The Protective Mother

The incest taboo has functioned historically and cross-culturally to prohibit sexual relations among designated kin.[44] Current information indicates that fathers, more than mothers, violate the incest taboo.[45] Mothers are expected to be "keepers of the incest taboo"[46] by protecting their daughters, not only from the sexual advances of the father, but from all other danger as well.

In contrast to this expected protective stance, the ideal woman in our society is socialized to be emotional, passive, dependent, and helpless; but she must also defend her children from harm. For a mother to assume a protective role on behalf of her children against their father would require her to behave in ways that are inconsistent with traditional female roles. Women have received few sanctions or opportunities for learning the dominant, assertive, restraining, controlling behaviors expected of mothers in incest-families. Because of this, many are caught in a no-win situation: to be a good, obedient wife is to be a bad, non-protective mother; to be a good, protective mother is to be a bad, disobedient wife.[47]

There are two tentative protective mother models. Suzanne Sgroi has outlined four characteristics necessary for any adult to act as a protector of a sexually abused child following disclosure: (1) belief that the abuse happened; (2) anger at the perpetrator; (3) belief that the perpetrator was responsible and should be held accountable; and (4) a lack of fear of the perpetrator.[48] Margaret Myer has looked at the balance of the mother's anger and empathy toward her husband and daughter as one of the factors affecting the mother's potential to provide post-disclosure protection for her daughter.[49]

A mother's capacity to protect her daughter has also been related to whom she chooses to believe and with whom she chooses to stay, her husband or her daughter. Judith Herman and Lisa Hirschman have suggested that some incest-family mothers seem to transmit a message to their daughters about why they chose to side with their husbands:

> Your father first, you second. It is dangerous to fight back, for if I lose him I lose everything. For my own survival I must leave you to your own devices. I cannot defend you, and if necessary I will sacrifice you to your father.[50]

Whom the mother chooses is thus seen as the basis for whatever protective or non-protective action she takes. Her choice has also been related to her passivity and powerlessness and her fear of and her dependence on her husband. But other possible contexts for her action have not been identified or explored. The mothers in this book demonstrated that choice for them was not necessarily a dichotomous matter and sometimes had little to do with power, fear, or their dependency on their husbands. For example, Cathy and Diane were each considering reconciliation with their husbands at the time I interviewed them, but each also chose to side with and did protect their daughters following disclosure. Their feelings about their family as a whole transcended their choice between two family members. Cathy expressed this well when she contemplated the way she believed other mothers made their choices:

> It's either going to be they're going to go on being married and forget about the kid or go on with the kid and have a divorce; one or the other. I don't feel any of these. To me the strongest feeling I have is wanting my family back together again without the fear.

Thus, we can see that a mother makes choices between her husband and daughter within a wider social context than just the mother's powerlessness. I do not intend to minimize the influence of sexist ideology, hierarchical power relations in the family, or a mother's access to alternative resources outside the family on the choice she makes. However, her choice may also be influenced by other factors: the age of her daughter at the time of disclosure; whether the daughter will still be in the home and will require further protection from the father; whether the mother feels the husband has been punished; whether there are leverages available to enforce new behavior in her husband; and whether her conditions for staying together are met.

Another issue that may be more strongly related to a mother's capacity to initiate and sustain protective action is whether disclosure is private or public and whether outside professionals with authority become involved with the family. None of the mothers I interviewed was able to protect her daughter alone. Ann and Diane tried to do so but were unsuccessful in stopping the incest from continuing in their families. The involvement of professionals with authority would appear to be critical in mitigating the father's authority, even when the mother experiences such intervention as intrusive, painful, and disruptive. But the involvement of professional outsiders alone will not be effective. The incest-family mother also needs the kind of ongoing, total life supports, as described by Suzanne Sgroi,[51] and the kind of reinforcement Diane received from her caseworkers to resist her husband's denial and distortion of reality. A mother has no power to punish her husband except to leave him or have him removed from the home, and even these two strategies leave the husband "getting away with it," as was the case with Diane's husband. So the mother also needs the leverage of the legal system to ensure some kind of punishment of her husband, the offender.

In conclusion, the mothers' capacity to protect their daughters suggests that the individual traits or characteristics of the incest-family mother will not necessarily influence whether she takes protective action or not and that the strategies she chooses will not necessarily determine how successful she is. Rather, the social context within which the disclosure takes place and the presence of outside professionals with authority may be the key factors that differentiate protective from non-protective mothers.[52]

There is a range of variability among the six mothers I interviewed for this book that suggests there may be even wider differences among the unknown universe of incest-family mothers. I do not believe mothers can be described simply as collusive, powerless, or protective. At the same time, the mothers in this book share things in common with each other and women everywhere. They belong to the sisterhood of women who have been socialized to assume their assigned position in society and the family and to perform their proper roles as wives and mothers. Much of their behavior and responses to the events in their lives are attributable to their positions in society and the family and the roles they have learned. In this sense, I have focused on the family and social contexts within which the incest event took place.

I did not set out to disprove any explanations or to offer any new theories about incest-family mothers. My goal was to listen to and to understand from a different angle of vision the six mothers who were willing to talk to me about their experiences and to tell me their stories. The tapestry metaphor used earlier serves to emphasize the complex and varied themes the mothers wove into their individual stories and highlights a new understanding of incest-family mothers.

In the final chapter I turn to the implications of this new understanding for those professionals who work with incest-families.

NINE

Notes to Professionals

I learned some useful things from the mothers who spoke with me that may be helpful to other professionals working with incest-families. While these notes are directed primarily toward social workers in public child welfare who are legally mandated to investigate and make dispositions on reports of suspected child sexual abuse, the suggestions are also intended for professionals of all disciplines who come in contact with incest-family mothers.

Developing a Helping Relationship

Social work has long placed importance on the client-worker relationship as the medium for helping and on an acceptance of the client as the keystone of this relationship.[1] Anything that contributes to the acceptance of incest-family mothers by professionals has the potential to create a climate where a relationship can be developed and nourished to facilitate, reinforce, and, when necessary, direct the mother's protective action on behalf of her daughter. A nurturing, supportive relationship will not only contribute to the mother's own growth and development but will also help her work toward healing the mother-daughter bond.

One of the most important things I learned from the mothers who spoke with me was their intense need to talk to someone who was interested in them, their feelings, and how the disclosure of the incest event was affecting them. They needed to know that they were not alone.

Workers in child welfare already hold a number of biased assumptions about incest-family mothers as basically collusive, which they have learned in part from the literature.[2] According to those in the field who have spoken with me, these assumptions are held by many professionals working with incest-families and are reinforced by a personal anger at the mothers because they failed to protect their daughters against the incest event. If workers in child welfare and other professionals can approach mothers with an openness and willingness to learn about the contexts of their lives and the experiences that lie behind the incest event, it may help them to be more accepting and understanding of mothers of incest survivors. The resulting helping relationship has the potential to provide a rich medium for helping.

Gathering Data and Assessment

Assessment is a collaborative process between the client and professional that includes a mutual identification and definition of the problem plus an understanding of the factors contributing to the problem, what the client wants to do about the problem, the strengths and limitations of the client, and the resources the client needs in order to deal with the problem. The incest-family mother's definition of the incest event, her explanations for its occurrence, and the meanings the incest holds for her are reservoirs of important information workers need to make comprehensive assessments. Mothers who feel they are accepted and understood will be more likely to provide information about the family context of the incest event with fewer defensive, self-protective behaviors, particularly when they are asked questions that allow and encourage them to describe their own subjective reality.

In a child welfare investigation, the assessment of the mother and the family tends to rest not only on the assumptions professionals bring with them but on the worker's interpretation of the mother's behavior at the time of disclosure. If she does not behave in the ways expected of a "protective mother," the worker is likely to dismiss her as a potential functioning adult ally for her daughter. For example, sometimes workers will direct a mother to behave in ways that conform to their own preconceived ideas about how mothers should behave in such a situation. Some of the mothers in this book who experienced the intervention of outside professionals resented being told how to control their feelings and how to respond to their daughters. Wanting to appear cooperative, and fearful of what might happen if they did not, they were inclined to follow directions and suppress the ways they did function well as mothers.

I used the ethnographic interview[3] to learn from the mothers in this book about their experience, and I believe it offers a useful model for interviewing and gathering data. The ethnographic interview has the facility to tap deeper levels of information and meaning about the incest-family mother's world as well as the different contexts of her behavior. Ethnographic questions are designed to explore and understand the symbolic meanings embedded in the ways people define their situations and describe their experiences. One of the reasons the mothers I interviewed were willing to talk to me was their need to go over what had happened in their families in an attempt to make some sense out of it, to understand it, and to find some meaning in it.[4] Instruction and experience in utilizing ethnographic questions in interviews offer professionals help to uncover hidden areas, to gather more detailed information, and to more fully understand the incest event. This approach has the potential to contribute to clear, mutually understood communication and empowers the client to become active in the helping process.

Two issues misunderstood by workers often prevent them from making a full, accurate assessment of the mother's capacity to act protectively on behalf of her daughter. These issues are the mother's previous knowledge of the incest event and her initial responses to the disclosure of the incest event.

A MOTHER'S PREVIOUS KNOWLEDGE

The assumption that "all mothers know" is not necessarily correct, and child welfare workers who equate "knowing" with collusion may unwittingly cut off a mother's potential to act protectively following disclosure. Therefore, it is important for workers to be sensitive to the different levels of a mother's knowledge of the incest event before disclosure and to differentiate among mothers who (1) actively fostered the incest; (2) knew about and condoned it; (3) suspected the incest but were unable to confront their suspicions; and (4) really did not know about the incest. It is also possible that the mother did know about the incest and attempted to take protective action alone or even with others, action that was not successful and did not stop the incest from continuing. It is important, and may be even more helpful, to understand the reasons why such attempted action was unsuccessful rather than blaming the mother for failing to protect her daughter.

Ethnographic questions have the potential to help workers explore deeper levels of the mother's level of knowledge and elicit important information about the family that can be used in the assessment process. For example, such questions would ask for the mother's knowledge of the behavioral indicators of incest; the different reasons why she may have been suspicious; the different reasons she was unable to confront her suspicions; the consequences she thought might ensue if she did confront her husband or ask her daughter; the different ways she might have dealt with her suspicions or retrospective knowledge; the reasons for not seeking outside help; and her expectations of outside help.

The answers to such questions offer rich data about a mother's perceptions and definition of the situation and are keys not only to the family dynamics and the context within which the incest occurred but also to understanding a mother's coping styles, problem-solving skills, and available support networks. Such information also provides insight into a mother's strengths, limitations, and needs and could become the basis of intervention programs toward informing mothers and other family members about incest and available resources.

A MOTHER'S INITIAL RESPONSES TO DISCLOSURE

The information from the mothers in this book supports Margaret Myer's conclusions that there may be stages in the process of the mother's responses to disclosure of the incest event.[5] Shock will sometimes masquerade as disbelief. A mother's inability to comprehend or understand incest as an event that really did occur in her family may produce a reaction resembling denial. Initial reactions change and do not necessarily portend a mother's ability to initiate or to sustain protective action. Initial disbelief and denial may serve to protect a mother from facing what she has to do: disrupt the family she believes it is her duty to preserve.

There are different reasons for a mother's disbelief and denial patterns and different ways in which a mother may express such feelings. Disbelief and denial are more than psychological defense mechanisms, and it is important for workers to understand the stages in the belief/acceptance cycle. Suzanne Sgroi has made a cogent point about a mother's retrenchment from initial belief to disbelief as she considers and realizes the consequences of siding with and protecting her daughter.[6] However, Sgroi did not consider a mother's responses in the opposite direction, from the shock of disbelief and emotional denial to belief and acceptance.

It is also important to understand the mothers' initial responses to disclosure within the context of the social service system. Mothers with little experience with community social services may not know what to expect. Other mothers with previous experiences may defend themselves against what they have perceived and felt to be the unhelpful intrusion of outsiders into their lives. Still other mothers may hold negative stereotypes about public agencies, as Bonnie did, making it difficult for them to trust that any offered assistance will be helpful. What professionals may interpret as defensive behavior around the incest event may actually be a mother's way of protecting herself against the feared intrustion of outsiders.

It is necessary and important for workers to follow the practice principle of clarifying with the mother what she can expect, what will and what will not happen, what workers and agencies can and cannot do, and to come to a clear, mutual definition and understanding of the client-worker-agency situation. Such an understanding will help workers to engage the mother's hope and facilitate initial contracting with her on how they will work together.

Intervention

It is difficult to assess from the statistics just how widespread the sexual abuse of children actually is.[7] And it is estimated that "Only one in every five cases is coming to the attention of professionals."[8]

It is equally difficult to estimate the number of incest-families where mothers have attempted to protect their daughters and how many of them were successful. I learned from the mothers who spoke to me that those who did attempt to intervene alone were not able to stop the incest from recurring in their families. The involvement of outside, professional authorities was necessary if the incest was to end. Yet the deeply held cultural value of family privacy still acts as a barrier against the intrusion of outsiders into the secrets of a family.

Several factors may contribute to keeping concerned professionals outside the family, other than the family's own social isolation and the protective boundaries the family constructs to keep outsiders out. Helping professionals are sometimes reluctant to intervene in the private crevices of family life and, when they do, are often left feeling that their intervention created more of a crisis for the family than the incest event itself, thereby diluting workers' confidence in their ability to help. Persons in the community are often reluctant to report their suspicions of incest because they foresee their report adding another level of devastation to the family, or because they do not trust or approve of what mandated professionals do when they receive a referral. Mothers and other family members may not seek outside help because they may truly feel they are able to stop the incest behavior alone or because they may have little confidence in community social and legal services.

One implication for primary intervention is the need to expand information directed toward parents and other family members about incest and other forms of sexual abuse. Present efforts include information on the behavioral indicators and the different signs pointing to possible incest. The dissemination of additional information about the availability of community services and support, what happens when a mother seeks outside help, and what the legal processes and alternatives are might help and encourage parents and other family members to report their suspicions of sexual abuse of children to professionals with some degree of confidence. But most importantly, we also need to let mothers know that no one expects them to protect their daughters alone and that support and help are available to assist them in doing what has to be done.

A second implication for intervention is the importance of professionals from different community systems working together cooperatively if they are to combat the sexual abuse of children successfully. A survey of professionals in the Boston metropolitan area who attended a series of conferences and meetings on child sexual abuse revealed that different agencies tended to operate alone and that there was a low level of cooperation among those agencies that worked with child sexual abuse.[9] Where there is a lack of cooperation and an integration of services, the efforts of all agencies are impeded.[10]

The third implication for intervention is the need to provide what Suzanne Sgroi has termed "total life support" services for the mother as she and the family move through the crisis following disclosure.[11] Mothers will need not only emotional support,[12] but concrete assistance in navigating and working with the professionals from the various community systems with which they will come in contact, such as public assistance, employment, child care, housing, police, the district attorney's office, the court, and the prison system if her husband is incarcerated.

The fourth implication for intervention calls for listening to the ways a mother explains the incest event. What she believes are the reasons why the incest happened, and how she defines the consequences for herself, her husband, her daughter, and the entire family, will indicate where the mother is and show the worker where to begin the intervention process. If professionals do not find out where the client is, intervention will never be more than in name only.

I have not addressed the wider contexts within which we must understand any intervention. Professionals work within agency systems, which in turn function within larger sociocultural, political, and economic systems. We cannot expect undertrained, underpaid, and overburdened child welfare workers to do what they are mandated to do without a strong, national, family policy and substantial economic and programmatic resources to back it up.

I have drawn some implications for professional practice from what I have learned from the mothers in this book as well as my own professional experiences. All the suggestions I have noted—developing a helping relationship, gathering data and assessment, and intervention—rest on a different set of assumptions about incest-family mothers and open new doors to helping them as individuals who function within a social and cultural context and helping their daughters and families as well.

The self-selected mothers in this study do not represent the possible universe of incest-family mothers. What has been true for them may not be true for other mothers. Until someone can find a way to locate and to seek understanding from mothers who (1) fostered the incest event, (2) did know the incest event was going on and did nothing about it, and (3) did not believe their daughters and actively sided with their husbands against their daughters, we cannot know or understand the possible different reasons for their behaviors. As professionals come in contact with mothers who demonstrate the behaviors above, some of the guidelines suggested from this study may help them unlock the door to understanding more about these mothers. More understanding may make it possible for child welfare workers to use their authority to help mothers who may be deeply caught in the web of victimization to learn new behaviors and realize their innate potential to grow beyond victims to survivors along with their daughters.

Social workers and other helping professionals play a role in the finishing work of the tapestry incest-family mothers weave. Professionals can begin to look at and understand the forces that shape the lives of women in our society, the social contexts of the lives of mothers, and set aside the widely held assumptions about wives and mothers generally and incest-family mothers in particular. Professionals can weave in support and direction and offer the hope of a different life for the mothers, their daughters, and their families. The source of the threads and yarns for this finishing work by professionals comes from listening to, hearing, and understanding the subjective reality of incest-family mothers and in knowing how to use themselves consciously and creatively in the intervention process.

Epilogue

Six years have passed since I interviewed the mothers in this book and it has been some months since I completed the last chapter. The mothers and their stories have been in my head for a long time now, and as I think about them I am struck by the realization that they are really very ordinary women, not unlike the mothers we all know and meet every day. And in many ways, the mothers in this book are just like those of us who are mothers. They are us; we could be them. As women we share a common experience, the experience of motherhood, even while the details of those experiences may differ.

After I completed this manuscript, I again contacted the six mothers to let them know that I had finished the book based on their stories and to find out where they were in their lives today. I did this with some of the same apprehension Lillian Rubin describes in her Epilogue to *Worlds of Pain*.[1] The mothers had all read the body of the original dissertation containing excerpts from their interviews and had approved of what I had written as accurately representing their experiences. And like the people Rubin had interviewed, they had found the reading painful. So I wondered how they would feel now, six years after they had spoken to me about their lives and their pain. Would they agree to having their words printed in a book available not only to the public but to their families and their friends as well? And I wondered what I would do if any of them would object to having their stories told to a wider audience. I was greatly relieved and encouraged that the mothers supported this book and still permitted their presence in it. They reaffirmed my hopes that this would be a book that would not only give professionals another side of the story about mothers in incest-families but offer help and hope to other mothers of incest survivors as well.

I was interested in knowing how the mothers experienced being a part of this study and what they thought about having such private, painful parts of their lives published in a book. Ann said that talking to me about the incest was an important part of her healing process. While somewhat hesitant about family members reading the book, "although they all know bits and pieces," she hopes her story and this book will help others by "fostering identification and hope. The public so often sees people as just case numbers; this person you read about is not someone you might know." The mothers in this book are women you might easily know and like.

Bonnie found that going over things with me helped her to resolve the residues of her own guilt about not knowing and therefore not doing anything about the incest; about being perceived by her daughter as being too weak to stop it. "She was a four-year-old who had to handle it herself." Bonnie said she now knows if her daughter had come to her she would have handled it. "I know I am a mother wolf who would protect her children from any harm." Yet Bonnie sadly admits her daughter did see her accurately in terms of how she behaved inside the home, but did not see the inner strength that Bonnie believes would have surfaced. Bonnie was enthusiastic about a book such as this being published, hoping it would help other mothers.

Cathy said our talks had helped her more than anything else because she could talk to me honestly about the way she felt, without the pressure she had experienced from others in the past to feel and say what they thought was appropriate. She was excited about her story being part of a book to help other mothers, to whom she sends a message: "At the time it is going on, you are devastated. You ask yourself, 'How am I going to get through this? How do I face this alone?' But this does not mean the end; there is a future." Cathy hopes this book will give other mothers the hope and strength to get through a similar situation if it happens in their lives.

For Diane, the interview was an outlet to get rid of some of the hatred she felt toward her husband and what had happened. "My hatred is gone now," Diane said. "If this book can help one person recognize what is going on, and will help prevent it from continuing, I'm all for it. It [a book like this] would make you feel you're not off your rocker, not make you feel so alone."

Ellen said talking to me helped her to survive and to get her feelings out. Ellen told me that the things we talked about, which she recalled almost verbatim, helped her to begin to improve her relationship with her daughter. Ellen believes this book is important. "Anything that can help any mother is wonderful."

Fay said, "It really helped me to talk with you. It helped me to put things in focus, to see things I might not have seen if I hadn't talked about it. As I look back now, I realize I was in a state of shock. I did not have time to think things out, although I think I handled things fairly well." Fay received individual and group counseling to deal with the aftermath of her discovery of the incest, and while she did benefit, she also felt the counselors did not demonstrate much compassion for her. "I got the feeling they were saying, 'If you were a better mother, you would not have let this happen.' I didn't feel they were really reaching out to me, saying, 'let me help you.'" Fay has looked for a book about mothers of incest victims in the library and bookstores and has found nothing. "I am glad there is going to be one, now."

As we conversed the mothers told me how their worlds have changed since the incest was disclosed and they had spoken with me. Today, none of them would describe themselves as they did when we first met—as devastated, shaken, broken, or empty. They are all survivors now, and have not only come through the incest experience to the other side, but in the process have grown into more assertive, self-confident women. Each mother said that she has dealt with the past and has put it away to live in today.

But what about their daughters? Unfortunately, not all of the daughters were doing as well as their mothers. The mothers reported their relationships with their daughters are "still good" or have improved, but they also said their daughters were not receptive to talking to them about the incest.[2] And what is the message in this for us? Couldn't the mothers carry their daughters along on the current of their own healing and growth? It would appear not. What barriers blocked the daughters from benefitting from their mothers' newly found strength and hope? We would hope that as mothers heal and find resolution, their daughters would as well. My own thoughts on these questions come from my work with incest survivors and from conversations with friends and colleagues who have either worked in this area or are themselves incest survivors.[3]

First, there is the issue of the mothers and their daughters not being able to talk to each other about the incest. Mothers and daughters universally have difficulty talking about less highly charged issues, and to expect that incest-family mothers and their daughters could talk about such a taboo, emotionally laden, painful family event as incest may be expecting more than any mother or daughter could do without considerable professional help. All the mothers did receive informal professional help around disclosure, but only three had engaged in any kind of formal counseling. And while most of the daughters were seen by professionals along the way, none of the mothers received counseling conjointly with their daughters.

Underlying the difficulty both mothers and daughters may have in talking about the incest, there is the matter of how such a subject is approached. The literature reports that some daughters claim they told their mothers about the incest while it was going on, only to have their mothers say, "But she never said anything to me." One way to tell something powerfully taboo, frightening, and painful is to couch the telling in language dressed up in disguises, which provides some degree of safety from actually confronting the feared subject. In this way the telling is not necessarily heard or understood and the whole matter is avoided. Mothers who are dealing with their own responsibility/guilt about the incest may do the same thing when approaching the subject with their daughters, and consequently they may not be as direct or clear in communicating their desire to "talk about it." Or, the timing may be wrong. Daughters may not always want to or be ready to talk to their mothers when their mothers are ready and want to talk to them.

Then there is the question about why the daughters' healing has not kept pace with their mothers' recovery. Aside from all the variables that affect the impact of the incest on survivors,[4] there are several issues underlying this question: the developmental timetable for healing, the difference between being inside or outside the incest event, the time required for healing, and the availability of professional help.

Developmentally, most of the daughters were not ready to deal with their trauma beyond the crisis help they received following disclosure. It appears that survivors are most likely to seek professional help when they are in their thirties. Ann's daughters, young adults in their thirties when I interviewed her, had sought ongoing counseling. And they initiated that help when more adult problems around intimacy, sexuality, and choice of partner had pushed them to it. Bonnie's daughter had also been in and out of counseling, but for issues other than the incest. The other daughters were all in early or late adolescence and they may need to wait for the next stage's developmental crises to emerge before deciding to work at a deeper healing level.

It should not surprise us that daughters will take longer to heal than mothers. Mothers and daughters are on different sides of the incest event. Mothers are on the outside. It did not actually happen to them, physically. It did not penetrate their bodies as it did their daughters who then internalized the abuse into their whole being. So the wound is deeper for the daughters, and deep wounds take longer to heal, requiring more time to exorcise the guilt and shame as well as the physical violation of their bodies.

And finally, competent, effective help is not always available or affordable when survivors of incest need it. And we must remember that there are still relatively few professionals who specialize in and have the training to work with the increasing numbers of incest survivors seeking help.

There is a lag between the recovery of the mothers in this book and their daughters. The mothers became empowered and found ways to escape the oppression of their husbands and to move on to become more independent. Their healing process was quite different from that of their daughters, probably because of their stage of development, and because they were outside the incest event, which made it an entirely different experience for them.

These are some of my own conjectures and we need to continue to look for answers to these questions in other directions. Hopefully, we have put the "collusive mother" to rest and we can concentrate on helping mothers and daughters to heal.[5] There are still more sides to discover to the story of mothers and daughters in incest-families. And we will have to wait for future studies to understand more fully the dynamics of this complex mother-daughter bond.

Appendix A
About the Study

DEFINITION OF TERMS

Incest does not mean the same thing to everyone. It is not only conceptually different from the overall category of child sexual abuse, even though the terms are often used interchangeably today,[1] but it differs in the ways criminal and child protection statutes among different states define what constitutes incest and child sexual abuse.[2] In this book I have used the following terms and definitions.

Father-daughter incest is defined beyond the exclusive criteria of genital penetration and biological blood ties and includes a range of sexual behaviors and any form of sexual activity that has to be kept secret between a father (an adult male in a position of paternal care, protection, and authority) and his daughter by blood, marriage, or adoption. This definition incorporates biological, legal, social, and psychological relationships.

Incest-family means that family group where the incest-family mother has acknowledged that the father-daughter incest has taken place. This widens the scope from other forms of verification by accepting the mothers' definition of the situation.

Incest-family mother means the mother by blood, marriage, or adoption who functions in the position of caretaker of the daughter involved in the father-daughter incest.

THE SAMPLE: LOCATING INFORMANTS

Incest is a highly taboo family topic that is a particularly difficult and sensitive area for researchers to study. Survivors of incest and incest offenders are, by and large, a "captive population" within the child welfare and criminal justice systems; they are therefore relatively accessible to researchers. Mothers of incest survivors are another matter. In order to study mothers directly, they must agree to be studied. But because they generally feel guilty and defensive, such mothers are not likely to volunteer to participate in research projects about the incest in their families, nor are they willing to talk about themselves.

I had worked as a social worker in the area of public child welfare for a number of years and had both personal and professional contacts within the social service systems of several communities. So I began my search for mothers of incest survivors with a high degree of confidence that I would be able to locate 20 incest-family mothers to interview through referrals from my colleagues. This did not prove to be the case, and I experienced many of the same difficulties of those who have gone before me in finding people who would be willing to talk about sensitive, taboo family topics.[3]

I began my search for mothers by calling the directors of public and private social service agencies in my own community, where mothers of incest survivors might be clients, to explain my research project. I then sent a follow-up letter along with a summary of my research proposal and a letter that their professional staff could give to any mother of a female, father-daughter incest survivor who met the following criteria: (1) the mother acknowledged that the incest had occurred between her husband and daughter and (2) the father and daughter were no longer residing in the same household. In this letter to the mother I introduced myself, told the mother what the research was about, solicited her participation, explained why I needed her help, and invited her to call me to schedule an appointment to meet me and learn more about the study.[4]

I also distributed this letter to the local Planned Parenthood office, Rape Crisis unit, Abused Women's Shelter, YWCA, and selected therapists in the community who were known to work with women, as well as posting it on grocery store bulletin boards throughout the community. Articles highlighting me, the study, and my need to locate mothers who would be willing to talk to me appeared in the local daily newspaper and the newsletters of the Women's Center and Family and Community Medicine residency program at one of the local hospitals. In addition, I promoted my study and need for mothers with professionals I knew in other communities who were working with incest-families.

Originally I hoped to locate at least 20 mothers to interview. Over a period of a year and a half, I could locate only six mothers of incest survivors. Four of the mothers were referred by persons who knew me personally; two mothers referred themselves, one after reading the newspaper article about my study and another after a friend showed her the letter I had distributed throughout the community.[5]

INTERVIEW PROCEDURES AND PROCESS

I began the interviews with a detailed explanation of the research to ensure the mother had a clear understanding of the study. This explanation covered the following topics: the objectives and goals of the research; what I expected from the mother; what the mother could expect from me; what the risks and benefits of her participation might be; how her rights, interests, and sensitivities would be protected; and how the findings of the research would be used. Such issues as confidentiality, anonymity, the logistics of the interviews, reimbursement for any expenses the mother might incur, and my legal reporting responsibilities were clarified.[6] I cautioned each mother that participation in the interview might prove stressful to her and informed her that I would not provide professional help during the course of the research. However, if deemed appropriate, I would refer her to another professional for help.[7] I also assured the mother that she could stop the interviews at any time.[8]

I taperecorded all interviews and transcribed all but the last one myself.[9] I took no notes during the interviews, but following each one I recorded my observations and impressions in a field journal, noting any striking nonverbal expressions or behavior from the mother during the interview; emerging themes, new questions, or anything that was new, different, or similar to the material provided by the other mothers; and my own behavior and subjective feelings. These field notes provided a rich context for the interviews as well as a framework of reference for organizing and analyzing the data.[10]

DATA COLLECTION: THE ETHNOGRAPHIC INTERVIEW

The goal of this study was to learn from and understand the meanings of the events in the lives of incest-family mothers from their points of view, to learn what they knew about their world and how they defined their reality at this point in time and within their various social contexts. The ethnographic perspective provided the best way to do this.[11] I have used selected aspects of the systematic, inductive procedures of ethnographic research to gather data about incest-family mothers and to analyze the meanings this experience held for them. This is quite different from the ways other researchers have studied mothers of incest survivors.[12]

Many of the assumptions and beliefs that society holds about incest are part of the web of larger shared cultural beliefs about familes, generational boundaries, the roles and responsibilities of parents, particularly mothers, and the incest taboo. These beliefs are deeply embedded in the feelings and values of researchers as well as the professionals working with incest-families and the general public. Many people are quick to define the world in which incest-family mothers live and the meaning that the incest situation has for them from their own conception of incest. The ethnographic perspective offers the opportunity to gain a wider understanding and definition of the situation from the vision and perspective of someone actually involved in that situation.

I used the ethnographic interview as described by James Spradley[13] to gather data and to learn directly from the mothers about the topics and issues that were important and relevant to them. This format allowed the mothers to initiate and tell their stories in their own way and proved to be a generative, topic-building process that they, rather than I, controlled.

The ethnographic interview may be thought of as a "series of conversations"[14] whose overall purpose is to learn from the informants. I began each interview with the question, "What is it like to be the mother of an incest survivor?" and was further guided by such inner questions as: What process does the mother use to go about describing her experience? What language, idioms, metaphors, phrases does she use? What causal and temporal connections does she make? What are her perceptions, perspectives, beliefs, and values? What is the meaning of the incest event to her?[15]

DATA ANALYSIS

According to James Spradley, the ethnographic interview and analysis proceed concurrently and each does not constitute a separate phase. Rather, the interview and analytic process comprise an overlapping feedback method, with each stimulating the other. For me, the data analysis did not prove to be as ongoing and evolving a process as I had originally planned. Nor was it as intertwined with the interviews as Spradley outlined. After using it intensively with the first mother, I found it to be somewhat too mechanical and unwieldy.

The analytic process actually evolved after the interviews were completed, in my immersion in the mothers' stories as I transcribed the taped interviews. I began to experience an intimate knowledge of the mothers from which I began to make intuitive connections between the mothers' stories, theoretical perspectives, and my knowledge of families and the incest phenomenon. As I read and reread the typed transcripts, categories, symbols, and themes began to emerge and crystallize. These categories converged into a pattern, and conceptual variations stood out within the categories among the different mothers, which I coded and organized into a series of matrices. I then organized this information around a conceptual scheme, which eventually developed into a holistic story that was both different and yet in some ways similar to the descriptions of incest-family mothers I had found in the literature. I then identified and collected excerpts from the interviews to illustrate the different parts of the story.

The two overall, dominant categories were the mothers' construction of their notion of family and the incest event. Subsumed in their construction of family were their ideas about and experience with family structure, relationships, roles, and intergenerational family themes. Incorporated in their construction of the incest event was a process from learning about the incest, through their emotional and behavioral responses to the disclosure, to the explanations they provided about the incest event and the meanings the incest held for them.

Finally, I developed a master matrix that showed the commonalities and differences among the stories of the six mothers. From this matrix I wove together the different perceptions, experiences, explanations, and meanings of the mothers into the story I have told in this book.[16]

STRENGTHS AND LIMITATIONS

Others have studied mothers of incest survivors.[17] Yet the findings from this study are "another country heard from"[18] because, to my knowledge, no one has shed their assumptions and entered the worlds of incest-family mothers to listen to, understand, and learn directly from their self-reports what their lives and experiences have been like. Herein lies the strength of this book.

On the other side of this coin of strength is the limitation of having information from only six mothers. How useful can this be for understanding mothers and the dynamics of incest families in new ways? Throughout this book I have addressed this issue to emphasize that we cannot generalize from the experiences of only six mothers to the yet unknown universe of incest-family mothers.[19] In addition, their very self-selection builds in an additional bias in favor of their subjective interpretations of their experiences, which is by no means the whole story but only *another* side of the story accepted up until now as the only story. So while the preliminary conclusions I have drawn must be necessarily viewed as only suggestive, they do generate hypotheses for future researchers to test. They are a tentative beginning to enlarge our vision of reality from the perspective of those who experience it and to see the relationship between this reality and the society and culture at large.

Another limitation lies in the methodology I used. The ethnographic approach, while most appropriate for the purposes and goals of this study,[20] is very time consuming in four areas. First, locating mothers to serve as informants required well thought-out strategies and constant follow-up with the identified sources for locating mothers. Second, because they were open-ended, the interviews themselves took hours of time in addition to the time I spent with the mothers when visits extended after the interview itself because the mother wanted to talk about issues not related to the incest event. And in some cases there were intermittent phone calls and ongoing contacts after the interviews were completed. Third, transcribing the taped interviews, while it served to immerse me in the stories the mothers told and the ways they told their stories, required endless hours of tedious, tiring work. And fourth, analyzing the interview transcriptions required intense and repeated rereading, coding, and organization of the wide range of topics the mothers presented into a framework within which to tell their stories.

The transcriptions of the interviews with the mothers who participated in this study hold many stories. Only one story is told here in this book. My own biases, assumptions, and theoretical perspectives have shaped this translation of what the mothers told me. The transcriptions of the interviews are available to other researchers who might find and tell a different story from the same data. Still others might analyze and offer different interpretations of the story I have presented here. This story can be assessed as one-sided. However, as concluded by Howard Becker:

> Each "one sided" story will provide further studies that gradually enlarge our grasp of all relevant facets.[21]

Appendix B
Letter to Mother

Dear Mother,

I am beginning a study about incest and am trying to find mothers of incest survivors to help me. Would you be willing to talk to me about yourself? You may find it helpful to talk with someone who is very interested in you and your feelings. I want to learn what this experience was like for you. I believe I can use what I learn from you to help other mothers who are going through the same experience. I also hope I can help professionals who work with families where incest takes place to understand the mother and these families better.

If you would be willing to help me, please call me at ——— and make an appointment to meet and talk with me about this some more. You may have some questions which I will try to answer. I will not tell anyone you called me and everything you tell me will be kept confidential.

I hope you will call me. I really need your help.

Most sincerely,

Janis Johnson

Appendix C
Initial Interview Protocol

A. Introduce myself.

B. Explain research project.
   1. What study is about.
   2. Purpose of study.
   3. Expected outcomes of study.

C. Overall plan of study.
   1. Extensive interviews.
      a. We will work together as partners.
      b. You will help me to understand what your experience has been like for you.
   2. Logistics.
      a. Time.
      b. Place.
      c. Expenses—child care/transportation.
      d. Taping and transcribing interviews.
      e. Privacy, confidentiality, anonymity.
      f. My reporting responsibilities.

D. Risks and benefits for you.
   1. May be painful—can stop, withdraw at any time.
   2. You will have someone who is interested in listening to you.
   3. You will be helping professionals to help other mothers.

E. Any concerns, questions about study or me?

F. Informed consent.
   1. Taping and transcription of interviews.
   2. Use of material from interviews.
   3. Return of tapes to mothers following completion of study.
   4. Opportunity for mothers to read part of study based on interviews with them.

Appendix D
Consent Forms

I have read Part IV, THE MOTHERS SPEAK FOR THEMSELVES, of Janis Tyler Johnson's doctoral dissertation, "An Ethnographic Study of Incest-Family Mothers" and give my permission for her to use the excerpts drawn from my interviews with her. I agree that such excerpts accurately represent my meanings and have not been interpreted in any way which distorts my experience.

I understand that the material in this dissertation may be used in the future as the basis for articles which may be published in professional journals; training workshops for professionals working with incest-families; and speeches to groups interested in understanding more about incest-families. I also understand that my identity and the identity of all members of my family will be protected.

_____   _____

Signature   Date

If there are any corrections, comments, or suggestions you would like to make, please note them below. Thank you.

I give Janis Tyler Johnson permission to use excerpts drawn from my interviews with her which are included in her book, *MOTHERS OF INCEST SURVIVORS: ANOTHER SIDE OF THE STORY,* to be published by Indiana University Press. I have read portions of the manuscript which include my words and agree that such excerpts accurately represent my meanings and have not been interpreted in any way which distorts my experience. I have also read the description of me in Chapter 2 and agree that it adequately protects my privacy and the privacy of my family.

_____   _____

Signature   Date

Notes

PREFACE

1. Rush, "The Freudian Cover-Up," 45.
2. Woodbury and Schwartz, *The Silent Sin.*
3. American Humane Association, *National Study on Child Neglect and Abuse Reporting.*
4. Murdock, *Social Structure.*
5. Kinsey, Pomeroy, and Martin. *Sexual Behavior in the Human Female.*
6. Watson, "A Hidden Epidemic."
7. See Finkelhor, *Sexually Victimized Children,* 9–11. Finklehor examines the political realignments that have taken place between the conservative moralists and the liberal professionals and academics as well as the shift of attention from the sexual psychopath abuser to the more familiar friend or family member abuser.
8. Ibid., 1–2.
9. Rush, "The Freudian Cover-Up." Florence Rush was the first to uncover the "Freudian cover-up." She pointed out that Freud retracted his initial seduction theory, which stated that repressed memories of disturbing, traumatic sexual events in childhood were causally related to hysterical manifestations in his female patients, for a more acceptable explanation: that such reports were neither true nor based in reality. This lay the foundation for Freud's Oedipal theory and gave birth to the belief that children, particularly female children, lie about being sexually abused. Jeffrey Masson has more fully examined and discussed the history and evidence of this issue in his book *The Assault on Truth.*
10. Russell, *The Secret Trauma.*
11. Finkelhor, *Sexually Victimized Children.*
12. See Goodwin, Sahd, and Rada, "Incest Hoax."
13. See Press, "The Youngest Witnesses," for an elaboration of how adults charged with sexual abuse are being acquitted and charges against other adults are being dropped. In the process of this new trend the veracity of children who say they were sexually abused is once again being questioned. Also see Heckler, *The Battle and the Backlash,* for an examination of this backlash of criticism that decries child sexual abuse investigations as "witch hunts" of "child accuse" and warns that child sexual abuse is threatened with a return to the closet.
14. Groner and American Lawyer Staff, *Hilary's Trial.*
15. Finkelhor, *Child Sexual Abuse,* 223–25.
16. Durkheim, *The Nature and the Origin of the Taboo.*
17. There have been numerous studies of mothers in incest-families, mostly unpublished doctoral dissertations, but most, with the exception of Heriot, are written from a psychological perspective. See Bennet,, "Father-Daughter Incest"; Harrer, "Father-Daughter Incest"; Heriot, "Factors Contributing to Maternal Protectiveness Following the Disclosure of Intra-Familial Child Sexual Abuse"; Kegan, "Attachment and Family Sexual Abuse"; King, "A Study of Mothers in Families Where Father-Daughter Incest Occurred"; Knudson, "Interpersonal Dynamics and Mothers' Involvement in Father-Daughter Incest in Puerto Rico." See also what are to my knowledge the only published studies that focus on mothers of incest survivors, Elbow and Mayfield, "Mothers of Incest Victims"; Faller, "The Myth of the 'Collusive Mother'"; Myer, "A New Look at Mothers of Incest Victims." Others, such as Butler, *The Conspiracy of Silence;* Finkelhor, *Sexually Victimized Children;* Forward and Buck, *Betrayal of Innocence;* Justice and Justice, *The Broken Taboo;* Maisch, *Incest;* and Tormes, *Child Victims of*

Incest have provided some vignettes of incest-family mothers within their general study of incest.

18. Elliot Liebow, *Tally's Corner* (Boston: Little Brown, 1976), 8.

19. See Finkelhor, *Child Sexual Abuse*, 26–27.

20. See Dietz and Craft, "Family Dynamics of Incest," for a study of protective workers' perceptions and attitudes about the role of the mother in incest-families.

21. See Berger, "The Credible Word." Berger writes about the ambiguity of "lived events," which never come alone but "entail many others." In order to understand any event, we have to acknowledge the ambiguities, both present and absent, that surround each event, and the unspoken dialogues (35–36).

1. INTRODUCTION

1. Masters, *Patterns of Incest.*

2. Fox, *Kinship and Marriage;* Murdock, *Social Structure;* White, "The Definition and Prohibition of Incest."

3. See Finkelhor, *A Sourcebook on Child Sexual Abuse*, for a review and evaluation of the research to date on child sexual abuse.

4. Cavallin, "Incestuous Fathers"; Gebhard, Gagnon, Pomeroy, and Christenson, *Sex Offenders;* Weinberg, *Incest Behavior;* Weiner, "Father-Daughter Incest."

5. Herman and Hirschman, "Father-Daughter Incest," particularly 737–39.

6. Rosenfeld, "Incest and the Sexual Abuse of Children," 92.

7. Lustig, Dresser, Spellman, and Murray, "Incest," 39.

8. See Caplan and Hall-McCorquodale, "Mother Blaming in Major Clinical Journals" and "The Scapegoating of Mothers," for a discussion of how mothers are blamed and scapegoated in clinical journals. See also Gavey, Florence, Pezaro, and Tan, "Mother-Blaming, The Perfect Alibi," which argues that we must "move beyond an implicit, if not explicit, mother blaming position" to seeing the family in a larger, sociopolitical context (23), and Rich, *Of Woman Born*, for a personal, historical, and cultural exploration of the institution of motherhood. See also Caplan, "Making Mother-Blaming Visible," and Surrey, "Mother-Blaming and Clinical Theory," for a further discussion of mother-blaming issues.

9. See the critiques of the research on incest by Chandler, "Knowns and Unknowns in Sexual Abuse of Children," and Katz and Majur, "The Incest Victim," which cite small samples, unsound methodology, conceptual fallacies, and sexist interpretations as flaws that make any findings questionable.

10. See McIntyre, "Role of Mothers in Father-Daughter Incest," and Wattenberg, "In a Different Light," for two articles that examine the role of mothers in incest-families from a feminist perspective. See also Jacobs, "Reassessing Mother Blame in Incest," and MacLeod and Savaga's section on mother-blaming in their article, "Challenging the Orthodoxy" (36–39).

11. See Elbow and Mayfield, "Mothers of Incest Victims"; Faller, "The Myth of the 'Collusive Mother'"; Heriot, "Factors Contributing to Maternal Protectiveness Following Disclosure of Intra-Familial Child Sexual Abuse"; and Myer, "A New Look at Mothers of Incest Victims."

12. Yvonne Tormes's study *Child Victims of Incest* is an exception. One can only wonder if the fact that Tormes was a woman influenced her to examine seemingly non-protective mothers from a social rather than an individual fault perspective.

13. Barry and Johnson, "The Incest Barrier," 489.

14. The reader who would like to trace this collusive mother theme can find a representative sample of mother-indicting statements in Barry and Johnson, "The Incest Barrier," 489; Cohen, "The Incestuous Family Revisited," 155; Cormier, Kennedy, and Sangowicz, "Psychodynamics of Father-Daughter Incest," 207;

Henderson, "Incest," 305, 307; Hersko, Halleck, Rosenberg, and Pacht, "Incest," 28; Justice and Justice, *The Broken Taboo: Sex in the Family,* 97–102; Kaufman, Peck, and Taguiri, "The Family Constellation and Overt Incestuous Relations Between Father and Daughter," 269; Lustig, Dresser, Spellman, and Murray, "Incest," 39; Machotka, Pittman, and Flomenhaft, "Incest Is a Family Affair," 98–100; Reimer, "A Research Note on Incest," 571; Rist, "Incest," 685, 687; Weiner, "Father-Daughter Incest," 612.

15. For a recent example of just this, see Waterman, "Family Dynamics of Incest With Young Children," 207. Waterman acknowledges that the profile she is presenting is only one of "many different ones which exist," but she does not follow through with any alternative pictures of incest-family mothers.

16. See Kathleen Koch and Carolynne Jarvis, "Symbiotic Mother-Daughter Relationships in Incest Families," for an up-to-date version of this symbiosis in families where father-daughter incest takes place.

17. Tierney and Corwin, "Exploring Intrafamilial Child Sexual Abuse."

18. Weinberg, *Incest Behavior.* For other examples of the use of psychoanalytic theory, see such early writers as Barry and Johnson, "The Incest Barrier"; Cormier et al., "Psychodynamics of Father-Daughter Incest"; Kaufman et al., "The Family Constellation and Overt Incestuous Relations Between Father and Daughter"; Kennedy and Cormier, "Father-Daughter Incest"; Lustig et al., "Incest"; Rascovsky and Rascovsky, "On Consummated Incest"; Sloan and Karpinsky, "Effects of Incest on the Participants"; Weiner, "Father-Daughter Incest."

19. Machotka et al., "Incest Is a Family Affair." See also Carter, Papp, Silverstein, and Walters, "The Procrustean Bed," for a feminist response to Pamela Alexander's "A Systems Theory Conceptualization of Incest," where the incest-family is described as a closed system. Carter et al. conclude that we cannot view the incest-family simply as a closed, isolated "system in a vacuum" (304). It is not the structure of the family system per se that sets the stage for incest, but the social and cultural contexts of the family that prescribe and reinforce patriarchal father/husband and submissive mother/wife roles (302).

20. Lustig et al., "Incest," 39.

21. Cohen, "The Incestuous Family Revisited," 256.

22. Maisch, *Incest,* 138. For descriptions of the controlling, tyrannical father in incest-families see also Cormier et al., "Psychodynamics of Father-Daughter Incest"; Herman, *Father-Daughter Incest;* Meiselman, *Incest;* Sloan and Karpinsky, "Effects of Incest on the Participants"; Tormes, *Child Victims of Incest;* Weinberg, *Incest Behavior.* For descriptions of the passive, helpless, submissive mother see Cohen, "The Incestuous Family Revisited"; Eist and Mandell, "Family Treatment of Ongoing Incest Behavior"; Herman and Hirschman, "Father-Daughter Incest"; Lukianowicz, "Incest"; Lustig et al., "Incest"; Weinberg, *Incest Behavior.*

23. See Herman and Hirshman, "Father-Daughter Incest." See also Yvonne Tormes's excellent study, *Child Victims of Incest,* which sought "to understand the circumstances associated with the failure of mothers . . . to fulfill their social role" (13) and found both mothers and incest victims describing the home as "an abode of constant fear and friction" (27).

24. Breines and Gordon, "The New Scholarship on Family Violence"; Dietz and Craft, "Family Dynamics of Incest"; Truesdell, McNeil, and Deschner, "Incidence of Wife Abuse in Incestuous Families."

25. Browning and Boatman, "Incest Children at Risk"; Lukianowicz, "Incest"; Tormes, *Child Victims of Incest.* The profile of the powerless incest-family mother is not unlike the profile of battered wives described in Dobash and Dobash, *Violence Against Wives;* Frieze, Knoble, Zomir, and Washburn, "Types of Battered Women"; Roy, *Battered Women;* Walker, *The Battered Woman.* In

many respects abused wives appeared to be traditional wives, also socialized into traditional sex roles and learned helplessness. For Wardell, Gillespie, and Leffler, these traits did not explain why so many wives were beaten since they did not differentiate abused from non-abused wives and assumed that beaten wives were deviant and somehow complicit; such a helpless profile blamed the victim for who she was. See their analysis in "Silence and Violence Against Wives." They call for the more "universalistic" analysis of William Ryan (*Blaming the Victim*) to direct attention to the structure of male-female relationships within a patriarchal society. Such an analysis might also more fully explain the powerlessness of the incest-family mother.

26. Herman, *Father-Daughter Incest*, 49.

27. Meiselman, *Incest*.

28. Herman and Hirschman, "Father-Daughter Incest."

29. Butler, *The Conspiracy of Silence*.

30. For a feminist analysis of incest see Butler, *The Conspiracy of Silence*; Conte, "Progress in Treating the Sexual Abuse of Children"; Dietz and Craft, "Family Dynamics of Incest"; McIntyre, "Role of Mothers in Father-Daughter Incest"; MacLeod and Saraga, "Challenging the Orthodoxy"; Taubman, "Incest in Context"; Truesdell et al., "Incidence of Wife Abuse in Incestuous Families"; Wattenberg, "In a Different Light." See also Jacobs, "Reassessing Mother Blame in Incest," for a feminist analysis of both mother blaming and power in incest-families and James and MacKinnon, "The 'Incestuous Family' Revisited," for a critique of the incest myths that have been accepted as facts, including the myths about the inadequate mother.

31. Rich, *Of Woman Born*, 247.

32. Finkelhor, *Sexually Victimized Children*, particularly 126–27 and 148.

33. McIntyre, "Role of Mother in Father-Daughter Incest," 466.

34. Weinberg, *Incest Behavior*, 172–215.

35. Meiselman, *Incest*, particularly 168–76 and 183–84.

36. Johnson, "Father-Daughter Incest."

37. Myer, "A New Look at Mothers of Incest Victims."

38. Others have done retrospective studies by examining case records. See, for example, Elbow and Mayfield, "Mothers of Incest Victims"; and Heriot, "Factors Contributing to Maternal Protectiveness Following the Disclosure of Intra-Familial Child Sexual Abuse." Faller's study "The Myth of the 'Collusive Mother'" drew data via clinical assessments of the mothers by professionals in different social service systems.

39. "Research Dispels Incestuous Family Myth," 3.

40. Ellenson, "Mothers Bear Some Blame for Incest?", 24.

41. In my own experience as a trainer with professionals of different disciplines I have repeatedly heard professionals express this anger toward mothers.

42. Myer, "A New Look at Mothers of Incest Victims."

2. MEET THE MOTHERS

1. For a description of the methodology I used, see Appendix A: About the Study.

2. I have roughly estimated the socioeconomic status of each mother's family based on their husband's or their family of origin's educational level, occupation, income, and life-style, along with each mother's subjective social class placement.

3. Adrienne Rich, foreword to *Working It Out*, Sara Ruddick and Pamela Daniels, eds. (NY: Random House, 1977), xiv.

4. Yet all the mothers I interviewed identified with the stories of the other mothers who particpated in the study. Ellen commented after reading chapters

3 through 7 that it was hard for her to realize that what the other mothers had said were not her own words.

5. Myer, "A New Look at Mothers of Incest Victims."

3. THE SECRET IS REVEALED

1. See Sgroi, *Handbook of Clinical Intervention in Child Sexual Abuse*, 17–21.

2. See for example, Herman, *Father-Daughter Incest*, 46–48; Machotka et al., "Incest Is a Family Affair"; and Sgroi, *Handbook of Clinical Intervention in Child Sexual Abuse*, 28–29.

3. Myer, "A New Look at Mothers of Incest Victims."

4. Sgroi, *Handbook of Clinical Intervention in Child Sexual Abuse*, 29.

5. Myer, "A New Look at Mothers of Incest Victims," 55.

4. KEEPING THE SECRET

1. See Herman and Hirschman, "Father-Daughter Incest," 745; Sgroi, *Handbook of Clinical Intervention in Child Sexual Abuse*; Maisch, *Incest*.

2. See, for example, Cormier et al., "Psychodynamics of Father-Daughter Incest"; Herman, *Father-Daughter Incest*; Kaufman et al., "The Family Constellation and Overt Incestuous Relationships Between Father and Daughter"; and Meiselman, *Incest*.

3. Weinberg, *Incest Behavior*, xx.

4. Groth, "The Incest Offender."

5. Ibid., 215.

6. See Brooks, "Families in Treatment for Incest." Brooks found that one common characteristic of the incest-families she studied was some type of marital violence.

7. Mildred Daley Pagelow, *Family Violence*, 81.

8. Herman, *Father-Daughter Incest*, 71.

9. Herman and Hirshman, "Father-Daughter Incest," 747.

10. Herman, *Father Daughter Incest*.

11. See Sgroi, Blick, and Porter, "Validation of Child Sexual Abuse," particularly 15–17 on secrecy.

12. Groth, "The Incest Offender," particularly the section on regressed offenders, 216–18.

13. Salvador Minuchin, *Families and Family Therapy* (Cambridge, MA: Harvard University Press, 1974).

14. See Rich, *Of Woman Born*, 226–37, for an examination of the mother-daughter relationship that has been "minimized and trivialized under patriarchy" (226).

15. See, for example, Barry and Johnson, "The Incest Barrier," Justice and Justice, *The Broken Taboo*; Lustig et al., "Incest."

16. Herman, *Father-Daughter Incest*, 81.

17. Ibid., 83.

18. Meiselmen, *Incest*, 129, and Brooks, "Families in Treatment for Incest."

19. Taubman asks, "What role does the father play in promoting or failing to resolve the mother-daughter hostility so commonly found in incestuous families?" ("Incest in Context," 36).

5. THE MOTHERS RESPOND

1. Finkelhor, "What's Wrong with Sex Between Adults and Children?"

2. Freud, *Totem and Taboo*.
3. Durkheim, *Incest*.
4. See Finkelhor, *Child Sexual Abuse*, 25, for a discussion of the "stepfather" risk factor.
5. Myer, "A New Look at Mothers of Incest Victims," 12.
6. Ibid.
7. Gelles, "Abused Wives."
8. Sgroi, *Handbook of Clinical Intervention in Child Sexual Abuse*.
9. Myer, "A New Look at Mothers of Incest Victims," 7.
10. Weinberg, *Incest Behavior*, xx.
11. Finkelhor, *Sexually Victimized Children*, 212.
12. Sgroi, *Handbook of Clinical Intervention in Child Sexual Abuse*, 29.
13. Gilgun, "Does the Mother Know?", 3.
14. Myer, "A New Look at Mothers of Incest Victims."
15. Sgroi, *Handbook of Clinical Intervention in Child Sexual Abuse*, 252.
16. Tierney and Corwin, "Exploring Intrafamilial Child Sexual Abuse."

6. EXPLANATIONS

1. Herman, *Father-Daughter Incest*. See particularly, Chapter 3, The Question of Blame, 36–49.
2. Conte, "Sexual Abuse of Children," 6–11.
3. See Butler, *Conspiracy of Silence*; Herman, *Father-Daughter Incest*; MacLeod and Saraga, "Challenging the Orthodoxy,"; McIntyre, "Role of Mothers in Father-Daughter Incest"; Taubman, "Incest in Context"; Wattenberg, "In a Different Light."
4. Herman, *Father-Daughter Incest*, 62.
5. Herman and Hirschman, "Father-Daughter Incest," 74.
6. Reimer, "A Research Note on Incest," 571.
7. Conte, "Sexual Abuse of Children," 8.
8. See Groth, "The Incest Offender," 225 and 229–30.
9. See Finkelhor, *Sexually Victimized Children*, 22; Groth, "Patterns of Sexual Assault Against Children and Adolescents," 5.
10. For different views of this particular intergenerational theme, see Finkelhor, *Child Sexual Abuse*, 181; Goodwin, McCarthy, and DiVasto, "Physical and Sexual Abuse of the Children of Incest Victims"; Myer, "A New Look at Mothers of Incest Victims," 56; "The Readers Write"; see Rich, *Of Woman Born*, 246–49, for a general examination of mothers passing on their own afflictions to their daughters; see also Strauss, "A Study of the Recurrence of Father-Daughter Incest Across Generations."
11. Diane's words echoed what I have often heard from incest survivors whose mothers had also been incest victims. Their mothers survived their pain by suppressing and discounting it, telling no one, receiving no help, and "getting on" with their lives. I could not help but wonder if a mother's cover-up and denial of her own incest experience might contribute to the way she perceived and responded to her own daughter's incest experience.
12. "The Readers Write," 24.
13. "Research Dispels Incestuous Family Myth."
14. Ellensen, "Mothers Bear Some Blame for Incest?", 24.
15. Herman, *Father-Daughter Incest*.
16. Finkelhor, *Child Sexual Abuse*, 26.
17. See particularly Groth, "The Incest Offender," 216–26, on the "regressed offender."
18. Tierney and Corwin, "Exploring Intrafamilial Child Sexual Abuse," 109–10.

19. Hersko, Halleck, Rosenberg, and Pacht, "Incest: A Three Way Process."

20. This is somewhat in contrast to the findings of Inger Sagatun, who studied how fathers, mothers, and daughters viewed each other's responsibility for the incestuous behavior. While all agreed the father was the most responsible, mothers felt they were more responsible than did other family members ("The Social Structure of Incestuous Families").

21. See particularly Herman, *Father-Daughter Incest*, 42–49; Justice and Justice, *The Broken Taboo*, 97–102.

7. MEANINGS

1. See Spradley, *The Ethnographic Interview*, for the "Use Principle," which states: "The meaning of a symbol can be discovered by asking how it is used rather than asking what it means" (156).

2. See Silver, Boon, and Stones, "Searching for Meaning in Misfortune," for a study of the function of finding meaning in childhood sexual abuse for the recovery of adult survivors of father-daughter incest.

8. SOME CONCLUSIONS

1. This is in the tradition of C. Wright Mills's "sociological imagination," that quality of mind that enables one to understand the relationship between the private, personal troubles of an individual and the public, social issues that lie within the structure of a society (*The Sociological Imagination*).

2. Harstock, "Political Change."

3. Blumer, *Symbolic Interactionism*; Meltzer, Petras, and Reynolds, *Symbolic Interactionism*.

4. Epstein, "A Different Angle of Vision."

5. Finkelhor and Baron, "High Risk Children."

6. See, for example, Browning and Boatman, "Incest Children at Risk," and King, "A Study of Mothers in Families Where Father-Daughter Incest Has Occurred."

7. See, for example, Eist and Mandell, "Family Treatment of Ongoing Incest Behavior"; Gilgun, "Does the Mother Know?"; Herman, *Father-Daughter Incest*; Kaufman et al., "The Family Constellation and Overt Incestuous Relations Between Father and Daughter"; Lukianowicz, "Incest"; and Machotka et al., "Incest Is a Family Affair," for different perceptions and opinions about whether the mother knows about the incest or not.

8. Ruth S. Kempe and Henry C. Kempe, *Child Abuse* (London: Fontana/Open Books, 1978), 66, quoted by MacLeod and Saraga, "Challenging the Orthodoxy," 36.

9. See, for example, Gilgun, "Does the Mother Know?"; Lukianowicz, "Incest"; and Myer, "A New Look at Mothers of Incest Victims."

10. See Gilgun, ibid., 3.

11. Contrary to other findings, Myer reported in her study "A New Look at Mothers of Incest Victims" that only one of the 15 rejecting mothers, none of the immobilized mothers, and nine of the 24 protective mothers admitted to being sexually abused as children.

12. See Koch and Jarvis, "Symbiotic Mother-Daughter Relationships in Incest Families," for a similar explanation for mothers' seeming denial of their daughters' sexual abuse, whereby the mothers "redefine their own incest experience" and "expect their daughters to do the same" (100).

13. Anna Clark, *Women's Silence: Men's Violence* (London: Pandora Press, 1978), 101, quoted by MacCleod and Saraga, "Challenging the Orthodoxy," 38. See also

Szegedy-Maszak, "Who's to Judge?", for the story of Dr. Elizabeth Morgan, who has been in prison for two years for refusing to reveal the whereabouts of her daughter in order to protect her from her ex-husband's alleged sexual abuse.

14. Wattenberg, "In a Different Light," 206.

15. See Finkelhor and Yllo, *Rape in Marriage*, for a review of current information about marital rape.

16. William H. Masters and Virginia E. Johnson, *Human Sexual Inadequacy*.

17. See Carnes, whose *Out of the Shadows* provides a framework for understanding child molesting and incest within the context of a sexual addiction.

18. Rich, *Of Woman Born*.

19. See Rich, ibid., Chapter 9, Motherhood and Daughterhood, 218–59, for a personal and theoretical examination of mothers and daughters within the institution of motherhood.

20. The dominance of the mother-daughter alienation and conflict theme was not always true, as exemplified by Smith-Rosenberg's "The Female World of Love and Ritual." Smith-Rosenberg writes of the relationships among females in the nineteenth century. She found, "An intimate mother-daughter relationship lay at the heart of this female world. . . . Expressions of hostility that we would today consider routine on the part of both mothers and daughters seem to have been uncommon indeed. On the contrary . . . the normal relationship between mother and daughter was one of sympathy and understanding" (15).

21. See Taubman, "Incest in Context," for a discussion of the association between mother-daughter estrangement and role reversal, which he claims must be viewed in its social as well as personality context, suggesting that the father's role be explored in this process.

22. See Koch and Jarvis, "Symbiotic Mother-Daughter Relationships in Incest Families," for a discussion of the symbiotic quality of the mother-daughter relationships in incest-families.

23. See Brooks, "Families in Treatment for Incest," for a comparison of the actual characteristics of incest-families with the sexual estrangement and role reversal stereotypes found in the literature. Brooks found no evidence to support these stereotypes.

24. See Finkelhor, *Sexually Victimized Children*, 26–27, for another perspective on role confusion.

25. See Groth, "The Incest Offender," for a description of two major husband-wife relationship patterns in incest-families: the aggressive/dominant husband who chooses a child-wife and the passive/dependent husband who chooses a mother-wife.

26. I want to thank Bambi Schieffelin for suggesting to me that perceptions of roles will often influence what behaviors will be accepted or tolerated. Also, see Evelyn Reed, *Woman's Evolution*, 3–22, for her discussion of the primitiive sex taboo as an incest taboo. She quotes from W. I. Thomas, *Primitive Behavior: An Introduction to the Social Sciences* (New York: McGraw Hill, 1937): " . . . among the Chagga they reinforce the sex taboo between brother and sister by making the sister the equivalent of the mother" (192).

27. See Gutheil and Avery, "Multiple Overt Incest as a Family Defense Against Loss."

28. See, for example, Tierney and Corwin, "Exploring Intrafamilial Child Sexual Abuse."

29. Macleod and Saraga, "Challenging the Orthodoxy," 38.

30. Sgroi, *Handbook of Clinical Intervention in Child Sexual Abuse*, 2.

31. Herman, *Father-Daughter Incest*, 62–63.

32. See Alsbrook, "Marital Communication and Sexism," for how this assumption connects societal and structural sexism to the politics of marriage, and

Ryan, *Blaming the Victim*, for a more universalistic analysis that would examine the institutional norms about the positions and roles of men and women and the ways in which society institutionally reinforces these norms.

33. See Safilios-Rothschild, "The Dimension of Power Distribution in the Family"; Heer, "The Measurement and Bases of Family Power"; Wardell, Gillespie, and Leffler, "Science and Violence Against Wives."

34. See Wardell, Gillespie, and Leffler, "Science and Violence Against Wives," who suggest socially learned male dominance and female subordinance alone do not explain why mothers appear powerless in the family.

35. Over the past century the structure of the family has changed. Most people would agree that the traditional, patriarchal family is giving way to a more egalitarian family form with fewer asymmetrical marriages and changing sex roles, both within and outside the home. Yet the second wave of the women's movement and the liberation of some women from gender-bound roles have not changed the social structure that still establishes and supports the legitimate authority of men over women. In the majority of husband-wife relationships the balance of power is still influenced by the culturally defined authority patterns and transmitted rules about the rights of males over females in the family. The private power arena of the family is still connected to the public power arena. For further discussion of these ideas, see Horkheimer, "Authority and the Family"; Weber, *The Theory of Social and Economic Organization*; Blood and Wolfe, *Husbands and Wives*; French and Raven, "The Bases of Social Power"; Gillespie, "Who Has the Power? The Marital Struggle."

36. See Truesdell, McNeil, and Descher, "Incidence of Wife Abuse in Incestuous Families," for a report of their study comparing the incidence of spouse abuse in 30 incest-families with spouse abuse in the National Study of Randomly Selected Families. They found spouse abuse to be more common in incest-families than in the general population. See also Brooks, "Families in Treatment for Incest," who found some form of marital violence to be a common characteristic in the incest-families she studied.

37. See Paula Johnson, "Women and Power," for a discussion of the indirect, personal, and helpless modes of power used by women. See also Thelma Jean Goodrich, "Women, Power, and Family Therapy," particularly the section on conundrums of power, 12–14.

38. See Wrong, "Some Problems Defining Social Power."

39. See Olson and Cromwell, "Power in Families."

40. See Russell, *The Secret Trauma*, 392–94 for a different analysis of incest as a sexual issue. Russel emphasizes the way male sexuality is socialized in this society. "Males are socialized to sexualize power, intimacy, and affection, and sometimes hatred and contempt, as well" (393).

41. See Rachel Hare-Mustin, "Sex, Lies, and Headaches," for a feminist postmodern theoretical examination of power.

42. I am grateful to Daniel Levinson for his "gender splitting" concept and his thoughts on this during the Cape Cod Symposium "The Adult Development of Women and Men," Eastham, MA, July 23–27, 1990.

43. See Breines and Gordon, "The New Scholarship on Family Violence."

44. While Murdock, in *Social Structure*, has claimed its universality, the incest taboo has exhibited variations among cultures in the definition of what constituted incest and the form of the prohibition. See for example Fox, *Kinship and Marriage*; Masters, *Patterns of Incest*; and Middleton, "Brother-Sister and Father-Daughter Marriage in Ancient Egypt."

45. See Finkelhor, *Child Sexual Abuse*, and Russell, *The Secret Trauma*.

46. See Fox, *The Red Lamp of Incest*.

47. This is reminiscent of the double bind theory (see Bateson, Jackson, and

Weakland, "Toward a Theory of Schizophrenia") used by Broverman, Broverman, Clarkson, Rosencrantz, and Vogel to describe the socially contrived double bind of women in our society ("Sex Role Stereotypes and Clinical Judgements of Mental Health"). Heriot sums it up: "To be a healthy woman by society's standards is to be a sick adult. On the other hand, for a woman to aspire to a social definition of adulthood is to do so at the cost of her womanhood" ("The Double Bind," 12).

48. Sgroi, *Handbook of Clinical Intervention in Child Sexual Abuse*, 93–94.
49. Myer, "A New Look at Mothers of Incest Victims."
50. Herman and Hirschman, "Father-Daughter Incest," 756.
51. Sgroi, *Handbook of Clinical Intervention in Child Sexual Abuse*, 104.
52. See Finkelhor, *Child Sexual Abuse*. He raises the question about whether unreported cases of child abuse differ from reported cases and suggests that future research on the process rather than the outcome of reporting would help to answer that question. There is still a lot to learn from mothers in families where outside authorities were not involved and about the process of reporting, investigation, and intervention from mothers who have been involved with professional authorities outside the family.

9. NOTES TO PROFESSIONALS

1. Perlman, *Relationship*.
2. Dietz and Craft, "Family Dynamics of Incest."
3. See Appendix A: About the Study for a fuller discussion of this methodology.
4. See Silver, Boon, and Stones, "Searching for Meaning in Misfortune," which explores the usefulness of searching for meaning in an adverse life event. While this article is concerned with adult survivors of incest, the discussion offers some useful insights into such a search for mothers of incest survivors.
5. Myer, "A New Look at Mothers of Incest Victims."
6. Sgroi, *Handbook of Clinical Intervention in Child Sexual Abuse*.
7. See Finkelhor, *Sexually Victimized Children and Child Sexual Abuse*; National Center for Child Abuse and Neglect, *Study Findings*; Russel, "Incidence and Prevalence of Intrafamilial and Extrafamilial Sexual Abuse of Female Children."
8. Finkelhor, *Child Sexual Abuse*, 232.
9. Finkelhor with Gomez-Schwartz and Horowitz, "Professionals' Responses."
10. Common Sense Associates, Inc., has developed and tested a community-based training model that includes a step-by-step plan on how to bring different systems in the community together to work cooperatively on behalf of sexually abused children and their families. See Common Sense Associates, *The Pennsylvania Model*.
11. Sgroi, *Handbook of Clinical Intervention in Child Sexual Abuse*.
12. See Koch and Jarvis, "Symbiotic Mother-Daughter Relationships in Incest Families." They note how incest-family mothers often have little "confidence in their ability to cope with life alone" (100), even when their strength and potential independence are evident. It is critical that incest-family mothers receive nurturance and emotional support form professionals to lessen their dependency needs on their husbands, their daughters, and other children in the family.

EPILOGUE

1. Lillian Breslow Rubin, *Worlds of Pain* (NY: Basic Books, 1976), 213.
2. While the mothers did talk about their daughters and of their relationships

with them, they still had the same kind of difficulty speaking about their daughters and the incest event that I remembered from the initial interviews. I felt that mothers were getting on with their own lives, leaving the past behind them, and they did not want to return to the pain of the incest. But I still had the feeling that they had not really been able to address the core issues of the incest with their daughters, as much as they may have wanted to.

3. I want to thank, particularly, Patty Coleman and Patricia Riley for their thoughts on these questions and their contributions to this section.

4. See Browne and Finkelhor, "Initial and Long-Term Effects: A Review of the Research," particularly 165–74, for a discussion of these variables.

5. See James and MacKinnon, "The 'Incestuous Family' Revisited: A Critical Analysis of Family Therapy Myths," for a critical, feminist analysis of the family therapy literature and an identification of several pervasive myths. One of the myths is the "pathological father and the inadequate mother."

APPENDIX A

1. See Sgroi, *Handbook of Clinical Intervention in Child Sexual Abuse*, 10–12 for a discussion about the further conceptual confusion that exists about the relationship of the incest perpetrator to the incest victim and the forms the sexual behavior takes; and Summit and Kryso, "Sexual Abuse of Children," for a typology of the different kinds of parent-child sexuality.

2. Bienen, "The Incest Statutes."

3. See Gelles, "Methods for Studying Sensitive Family Topics," for a good discussion of the special problems in sensitive-area research and some proposed ways to study taboo subjects.

4. See Appendix B: Letter to Mother.

5. I believe that the mothers who were willing to participate in this study did so primarily because they trusted the person who referred them. This is an important point when the researcher is depending upon others for referrals. It means ground work must be done with the referral source. The way she or he presents the research to potential informants, the degree to which they believe in the importance of the research, and their feelings about the researcher will all have influential power on the potential informant's decision to participate or not. This, of course, is in addition to the relationship between the referral source and her or his client.

6. See Appendix C: Initial Interview Protocol, and Appendix D: Consent Forms.

7. I did make such a referral with one mother.

8. I was seldom able to complete this initial part of the interview before the mother would begin to tell me her story. However, some of these issues would occasionally come up in the course of the interviews, at which time I would again discuss and clarify them.

9. I enlisted the assistance of a professional typist who had experience transcribing recorded dictation in a professional agency to help me at the end. However, she did not transcribe any interviews with mothers who resided in her community. After the dissertation was completed, I gave each mother the tapes of her interviews with me.

10. See Bogdon and Taylor, *Introduction to Qualitative Research Methods*, 118–19.

11. For a fuller explanation of the ethnographic perspective, see Agar, "Getting Better Quality Stuff"; Geertz, "From the Native's Point of View"; Geertz, *The Interpretation of Culture*; and Hymes, "What is Ethnography?"

12. See note 17, Preface.

13. Spradley, *The Ethnographic Interview.*

14. Ibid., 58.

15. The reader who is interested in learning more about the structure of the different kinds of ethnographic questions and the parallel process of ethnographic analysis will find a clear, guided learning experience in Spradley, *The Ethnographic Interview.*

16. This analytic process is very difficult to describe. The reader who is interested will find a more detailed description in Spradley, *The Ethnographic Interview,* and will be able to see how I adapted Spradley's analytic process.

17. See note 17, Preface.

18. Geertz, *The Interpretation of Culture,* 23.

19. Considering the available data about the projected prevalence of child sexual abuse by a family member, we can only speculate on the wide variety of experiences within incest-families.

20. See Filstead, *Qualitative Methodology,* for a wide range of readings on qualitative research.

21. Becker, *Sociological Work,* 134.

References

Agar, Michael. "Getting Better Quality Stuff." *Urban Life* 9 (1980): 34–50.

Alexander, Pamela. "A Systems Conceptualization of Incest." *Family Process* 24 (1985): 79–88.

Allen, Charlotte V. *Daddy's Girl*. NY: Simon and Schuster, 1980.

Alsbrook, Larry. "Marital Communication and Sexism." *Social Casework* 57 (1976): 517–22.

American Humane Association. *National Study on Child Neglect and Abuse Reporting*. Denver: American Humane Association, 1981.

Armstrong, Louise. Kiss Daddy Goodnight. NY: Hawthorn, 1978.

Barry, Maurice J., and Adelaide M. Johnson. "The Incest Barrier." *Psychoanalytic Quarterly* 27 (1976): 485–500.

Bass, Ellen, and Louise Thornton, eds. *I Never Told Anyone: Writings by Women Survivors of Child Sexual Abuse*. NY: Harper and Row, 1983, Colophon Books.

Bateson, Gregory, Don Jackson, and John Weakland. "Toward a Theory of Schizophrenia." *Behavioral Science* 1 (1956): 251–64.

Becker, Howard. *Sociological Work: Method and Substance*. Brunswick, NJ: Transaction Books, 1970.

Bennett, Michael H. "Father-Daughter Incest: A Psychological Study of the Mother from an Attachment Theory Perspective." Ph.D. diss., California School of Professional Psychology, 1980.

Berger, John. "The Credible Word." *Harpers Magazine*, July 1988, 35.

Bernard, Jessie. *Women, Wives, and Mothers: Values and Options*. Chicago: Aldine, 1975.

Bienen, Leigh, B. "The Incest Statutes." In *Father-Daughter Incest*, Judith Herman, 221–59. Cambridge, MA: Harvard University Press, 1981.

Blood, Robert O., Jr., and Donald M. Wolfe. *Husbands and Wives*. NY: Free Press, 1960.

Blumer, Herbert. *Symbolic Interactionism. Perspective and Method*. Englewood Cliffs, NJ: Prentice-Hall, 1969.

Bogdon, Robert, and Steven J. Taylor. *Introduction to Qualitative Methods: A Phenomenological Approach to the Social Sciences*. NY: John Wiley, 1975.

Brady, Katherine. *Father's Days*. NY: Seaview Books, 1979; Dell, 1981.

Breines, Wini, and Linda Gordon. "The New Scholarship on Family Violence." *Signs* 8 (1983): 490–531.

Brooks, Barbara. "Families in Treatment for Incest." Ph.D. diss., University of Massachusetts, 1981.

Broverman, Inge K., Donald M. Broverman, Frank E. Clarkson, Paul S. Rosencrantz, and Susan R. Vogel. "Sex Role Stereotypes and Clinical Judgements of Mental Health." *Journal of Consulting and Clinical Psychology* 34 (1970): 1–7.

Browne, Angela, and David Finkelhor. "Initial and Long Term Effects: A Review of the Research." In *A Sourcebook on Child Sexual Abuse*, David Finkelhor and Associates, 180–98. Beverly Hills, CA: Sage, 1986.

Browning, Diane J., and Bonnie Boatman. "Incest: Children at Risk." *American Journal of Psychiatry* 134 (1977): 69–72.

Butler, Sandra. *Conspiracy of Silence: The Trauma of Incest*. San Francisco: New Glide, 1978.

Caplan, Paula J. "Making Mother-Blaming Visible: The Emperor's New Clothes." In *Woman-Defined Motherhood*, Jane Price Knowles and Ellen Cole, eds., 61–70. Binghamton, NY: Harrington Park Press, 1990.

Caplan, Paula J., and Ian Hall-McCorquodale. "Mother-Blaming in Major Clinical Journals." *American Journal of Orthopsychiatry* 55 (1985): 345–52.

———. "The Scapegoating of Mothers: A Call for Change." *American Journal of Orthopsychiatry* 55 (1985): 610–13.

Carnes, Patrick. *Out of the Shadows: Understanding Sexual Addiction.* Minneapolis, MN: CompCare, 1983.

Carter, Betty, Peggy Papp, Olga Silverstein, and Marianne Walters. "The Procrustean Bed." *Family Process* 25 (1986): 301–304.

Cavallin, Hector. "Incestuous Fathers: A Clinical Report." *American Journal of Psychiatry* 122 (1966): 1132–38.

Chandler, Susan Myers. "Knowns and Unknowns in Sexual Abuse of Children." *Journal of Social·Work and Human Sexuality* 1 (1982): 51–68.

Cohen, Tamar. "The Incestuous Family Revisited." *Social Casework* 64 (1983): 154–61.

Common Sense Associates, Inc. *The Pennsylvania Model: A Guide for Responding to Child Sexual Abuse.* 208 West Main Street, Mechanicsburg, PA 19055, 1987.

Conte, Jon R. "Sexual Abuse of Children: Enduring Issues for Social Work." *Journal of Social Work and Human Sexuality* 1 (1982): 1–20.

———. "Progress in Treating Sexual Abuse of Children." *Social Work* 29 (1984): 258–63.

Cormier, Bruno M., Miriam Kennedy, and Jadwiga Sangowitz. "Psychodynamics of Father Daughter Incest." *Canadian Psychiatric Association Journal* 7 (1962): 203–17.

Dietz, Christine A., and John L. Craft. "Family Dynamics of Incest: A New Perspective." *Social Casework* 61 (1980): 602–609.

Dobash, R. Emerson, and Russell Dobash. *Violence Against Wives.* NY: Free Press, 1979.

Durkheim, Emile. *Incest: The Nature and Origin of the Taboo.* NY: L. Stuart, 1963 (originally published 1897).

Eist, Harold I., and Adeline U. Mandell. "Family Treatment of Ongoing Incest Behavior." *Family Process* 7 (1968): 216–32.

Elbow, Margaret, and Judy Mayfield. "Mothers of Incest Victims: Villians, Victims, or Protectors?" *Families in Society* 72 (1991): 78–84.

Ellenson, Gerald S. "Mothers Bear Some Blame for Incest?" (The Readers Write). *NASW News*, May 1984, 24.

Epstein, Cynthia. "A Different Angle of Vision: Notes on the Selective Eye of Sociology." *Social Science Quarterly* 55 (1974): 645–56.

Faller, Kathleen Coulborn. "The Myth of the 'Collusive Mother.'" *Journal of Interpersonal Violence* 3 (1988): 190–96.

Filstead, William J. *Qualitative Methodology: Firsthand Involvement with the Social World.* Chicago: Markham, 1970.

Finkelhor, David. *Sexually Victimized Children.* NY: Free Press, 1979.

———. "What's Wrong with Sex Between Adults and Children?" *American Journal of Orthopsychiatry* 49 (1979): 692–97.

———. *Child Sexual Abuse: New Theory and Research.* NY: Free Press, 1984.

Finkelhor, David, and Associates. *A Sourcebook on Child Sexual Abuse.* Beverly Hills, CA: Sage, 1986.

Finkelhor, David, and Larry Baron. "High Risk Children." In David Finkelhor and Associates, *A Sourcebook on Child Sexual Abuse*, 60–88. Beverly Hills, CA: Sage, 1986.

Finkelhor, David, with Beverly Gomez-Schwartz and Jonathan Horowitz. "Professionals' Response." In *Child Sexual Abuse: New Theory and Research*, David Finkelhor, 200–20. NY: Free Press, 1984.

Finkelhor, David, and Kersti Yllo. "Rape in Marriage: A Sociological View." In *The Dark Side of Families,* David Finkelhor, Richard Gelles, Gerald Hotaling, and Murray Strau, eds., 119–31. Beverly Hills, CA: Sage, 1983.

Forward, Susan, and Craig Buck. *Betrayal of Innocence: Incest and Its Devastation.* NY: Penguin Books, 1979.

Fox, Robin. *Kinship and Marriage.* Middlesex, England: Penguin Books Ltd., Pelican Books, 1967.

———. *The Red Lamp of Incest.* NY: E. P. Dutton, 1980.

French, John R. P., Jr., and Bertram Raven. "The Bases of Social Power." In *Studies in Social Power,* D. Cartwright, Ed., 150–67. Ann Arbor: Research Center for Group Dynamics, 1959.

Freud, Sigmund. *Totem and Taboo.* NY: W. W. Norton, 1952.

Frieze, Irene Hanson, Jaime Knoble, Gretchen Zomnir, and Carol Washburn. "Types of Battered Women." Paper presented at the Annual Research Conference of the Association for Women in Psychology. Santa Monica, CA, 1980.

Gavey, Nicola, Joy Florence, Sue Pezaro, and Jan Tan. "Mother-Blaming, the Perfect Alibi: Family Therapy and the Mothers of Incest Victims." *Journal of Feminist Family Therapy* 2 (1990): 1–25.

Gebhard, Paul, J. H. Gagnon, W. B. Pomeroy, and C. V. Christenson. *Sex Offenders: An Analysis of Types.* NY: Harper and Row, 1965.

Geertz, Clifford. *The Interpretation of Culture.* NY: Basic Books, 1973.

———. "From the Native's Point of View: The Nature of Anthropological Understanding." In *Meaning in Anthropology,* K. H. Basso and H. A. Selby, eds., 221–37. Albuquerque: University of New Mexico Press, 1976.

Gelles, Richard J. "Abused Wives: Why Do They Stay?" *Journal of Marriage and the Family* 38 (1976): 659–68.

———. "Methods for Studying Sensitive Family Topics." *American Journal of Orthopsychiatry* 48 (1978): 408–24.

Gilgun, Janet F. "Does the Mother Know? Alternatives to Blaming Mothers for Child Sexual Abuse." *Response* 7 (Fall 1984): 2–4.

Gillespie, Dair L. "Who Has the Power? The Marital Struggle." *Journal of Marriage and the Family* 33 (1971): 445–58.

Goodrich, Thelma Jean. "Women, Power, and Family Therapy: What's Wrong With This Picture?" *Journal of Feminist Family Therapy* 3 (1991): 1–37.

Goodwin, Jean, Terista McCarty, and Peter DiVasto. "Physical and Sexual Abuse of the Children of Adult Incest Victims." In *Sexual Abuse: Incest Victims and their Families,* Jean Goodwin, 139–54. Boston: John Wright, 1982.

Goodwin, Jean, Doris Sahad, and Richard Rada. "Incest Hoax: False Accusations, False Denials." *Bulletin of the American Academy of Psychiatry and Law* 6 (1979): 269–76.

Groner, Jonathan. *Hilary's Trial: The Elizabeth Morgan Case and the Betrayal of Our Children by America's Legal System.* NY: American Lawyer Books/ Simon and Schuster, 1991.

Groth, Nicholas A. "Patterns of Sexual Assault Against Children and Adolescents." In *Sexual Assault of Children and Adolescents,* Ann Burgess, Nicholas Groth, Lynn Holstrom, and Suzanne Sgroi, 3–24. Lexington, MA: Lexington Books, 1978.

———. "The Incest Offender." In *Handbook of Clinical Intervention in Child Sexual Abuse,* Suzanne M. Sgroi, 215–39. Lexington, MA: Lexington Books, 1982.

Gutheil, Thomas O., and Nicholas C. Avery. "Multiple Overt Incest as a Family Defense Against Loss." *Family Process* 16 (1977): 105–16.

Hare-Mustin, Rachel T. "Sex, Lies, and Headaches: The Problem Is Power." *Journal of Feminist Family Therapy* 3 (1991): 39–61.

Harrer, Margaret N. "Father-Daughter Incest: A Study of the Mother." Ph.D. diss., Indiana University, 1980.

Harstock, Nancy. "Political Change: Two Perspectives on Power." *Quest* 1 (1974): 10–25.

Heckler, Davis. *The Battle and the Backlash: The Child Sexual Abuse War.* Lexington, MA: Heath, 1987.

Heer, David. "The Measurement and Bases of Family Power: An Overview." *Marriage and Family Living* 25 (1963): 113–39.

Henderson, James D. "Incest: A Synthesis of Data." *Canadian Psychiatric Association Journal* 17 (1972): 299–314.

Heriot, Jessica. "The Double Bind: Healing the Split." In *Women Changing Therapy*, J. Hammermon and R. Siegel, eds., 11–28. NY: Haworth, 1983.

———. "Factors Contributing to Maternal Protectiveness Following the Disclosure of Intra-Familial Child Sexual Abuse: A Documentary Study Based on Reports of Child Protective Service Workers." Ph.D. diss., School of Social Work and Community Planning, 1991.

Herman, Judith L. *Father-Daughter Incest.* Cambridge, MA: Harvard University Press, 1981.

Herman, Judith L., and Lisa Hirshman. "Father-Daughter Incest." *Signs* 2 (1977): 735–56.

———. "Father-Daughter Incest: A Clinical Study." Final Report. Rockville, MD: National Center for the Prevention and Control of Rape, 1978. Photocopied.

Hersko, Marvin, Seymour Halleck, Marshall Rosenburg, and Asher R. Pacht. "Incest: A Three Way Process." *Journal of Social Therapy* 7 (1961): 22–31.

Horkheimer, Max. "Authority and the Family." In *Critical Theory: Selected Essays*, 47–129. NY: Herder and Herder, 1972.

Hymes, Dell. "What is Ethnography?" In *Children In and Out of School: Ethnograpy and Education*, P. Gilmore and A. A. Glatthorn, eds., 21–32. Series/ 2, 1982.

Jacobs, Janet L. "Reassessing Mother Blame in Incest." *Signs* 15 (1990): 500–14.

James, Kerrie, and Laurie MacKinnon. "The 'Incestuous Family' Revisited: A Critical Analysis of Family Therapy Myths." *Journal of Marital and Family Therapy* 16 (1990): 71–88.

Johnson, Janis T. "Father-Daughter Incest: An Exploratory Study." Unpublished manuscript, University of Pennsylvania, 1978.

Johnson, Paula. "Women and Power: Toward a Theory of Effectiveness." *Journal of Social Issues* 32 (1976): 99–100.

Justice, Blair, and Rita Justice. *The Broken Taboo: Sex in the Family.* NY: Human Science Press, 1979.

Katz, S., and M. Majur. "The Incest Victim." In *Understanding the Rape Victim*, 249–84. NY: John Wiley and Sons, 1979.

Kaufman, Irving, Alice L. Peck, and Consuelo K. Taguiri. "The Family Constellation and Overt Incestuous Relations Between Father and Daughter." *American Journal of Orthopsychiatry* 24 (1954): 266–79.

Kegan, Katherine Anne. "Attachment and Family Sexual Abuse: An Investigation of the Families of Origin and Social Histories of Mothers from Present Incest Families." Ph.D. diss., University of Minnesota, 1981.

Kennedy, M., and B. M. Cormier. "Father-Daughter Incest: Treatment of the Family." *Laval Medical* 40 (1969): 946–50.

King, Harvey Wellman. "A Study of Mothers in Families Where Father-Daughter Incest Has Occurred." Ph.D. diss., California School of Professional Psychology, 1985.

Kinsey, Alfred C., Wordell B. Pomeroy, Clyde E. Martin, and Paul H. Gebhard. *Sexual Behavior in the Human Female.* Philadelphia: Saunders, 1953.

Knudson, Doris Gonzalez. "Interpersonal Dynamics and Mothers' Involvement in Father-Daughter Incest in Puerto Rico." Ph.D. diss., Ohio State University, 1981.

Koch, Kathleen, and Carolynne Jarvis. "Symbiotic Mother-Daughter Relationships in Incest Families." *Social Casework* 68 (1987): 94–101.

Lukianowicz, Narcyz. "Incest." *British Journal of Psychiatry* 120 (1972): 301–13.

Lustig, Noel, John W. Dresser, Seth W. Spellman, and Thomas B. Murray. "Incest: A Family Group Survival Pattern." *Archives of General Psychiatry* 14 (1966): 31–40.

MacCleod, Mary, and Esther Saraga. "Challenging the Orthodoxy: Towards a Feminist Theory." *Feminist Review* 28 (Spring 1988): 16–55.

Machotka, Pavel, Frank Pittman, and Kalman Flomenhaft. "Incest Is a Family Affair." *Family Process* 6 (1967): 98–116.

Maisch, Herbert. *Incest.* NY: Stein and Day, 1972.

Masson, Jeffrey M. *The Assault on Truth: Freud's Suppression of the Seduction Theory.* NY: Farrar, Straus and Girous, 1983.

Masters, R. E. L. *Patterns of Incest.* NY: Julian Press, 1963.

Masters, William H., and Virginia E. Johnson. *Human Sexual Inadequacy.* Boston: Little Brown, 1970.

McIntyre, Kevin. "Role of Mothers in Father-Daughter Incest: A Feminist Analysis." *Social Work* 26 (1981): 462–67.

Meiselman, Karin C. *Incest.* San Francisco: Jossey-Bass, 1978.

Meltzer, Bernard N., John W. Petras, and Larry T. Reynolds. *Symbolic Interactionism: Genesis, Varieties and Criticism.* Boston: Routledge and Kegan Paul, 1975.

Middleton, Russell. "Brother-Sister and Father-Daughter Marriage in Ancient Egypt." *American Sociological Review* 27 (1962): 603–11.

Mills, C. Wright. *The Sociological Imagination.* NY: Oxford University Press, 1959.

Murdock, George. *Social Structure.* NY: Macmillan, 1949.

Myer, Margaret. "A New Look at Mothers of Incest Victims." *Journal of Social Work and Human Sexuality* 3 (1984/85). 47–58.

National Center for Child Abuse and Neglect (NCCAN). "Study Findings: National Study of Incidence and Severity of Child Abuse and Neglect." Washington, D.C.: DHEW, 1981.

Olson, David H., and Ronald E. Cromwell. "Power in Families." In *Power in Families,* Ronald E. Cromwell and David H. Olson, eds., 3–14. NY: John Wiley and Sons, 1975.

Pagelow, Mildred Daley. *Family Violence.* New York: Praeger, 1984.

Perlman, Helen Harris. *Relationship: The Heart of Helping People.* Chicago: University of Chicago Press, 1979.

Press, Aric. "The Youngest Witnesses." *Newsweek,* February 18, 1985, 72.

Rascovsky, Matilde Wencelblat, and Arnaldo Rascovsky. "On Consummated Incest." *International Journal of Psychoanalysis* 31 (1950): 42–47.

Reed, Evelyn. *Woman's Evolution.* NY: Pathfinder Press, 1975.

Reimer, Svend. "A Research Note on Incest." *American Journal of Sociology* 45 (1940): 566–75.

"Research Dispels Incestuous Family Myth." *NASW News,* March 1984, 3.

Rich, Adrienne. *Of Woman Born: Motherhood as Experience and Institution.* NY: Bantam Books, 1977; first published W. W. Norton, 1976.

Rist, Kate. "Incest: Theoretical and Clinical Views." *American Journal of Orthopsychiatry* 49 (1979): 680–91.

Rosenfeld, Alvin A. "Incest and the Sexual Abuse of Children." *Journal of American Academy of Child Psychiatry* 16 (1977): 327–39.

Roy, Maria, ed. *Battered Women.* NY: Van Nostrand Reinhold, 1977.

Rush, Florence. "The Freudian Cover-Up." *Chrysalis* 1 (1977): 31–45.
———. *The Best Kept Secret.* NY: Prentice-Hall, 1980.
Russell, Diana. "Incidence and Prevalence of Intrafamilial and Extrafamilial Sexual Abuse of Female Children." *Child Abuse and Neglect* 7 (1983): 133–46.
———. *The Secret Trauma.* NY: Basic Books, 1986.
Ryan, William. *Blaming the Victim.* NY: Vintage Books, 1981.
Safilios-Rothschild, Constantina. "The Dimensions of Power Distribution in the Family." In *Marriage: Structure Dynamics and Therapy*, H. Gruenbaum and J. Christ, eds., 275–92. Boston: Little Brown, 1976.
Sgroi, Suzanne. *Handbook of Clinical Intervention in Child Sexual Abuse.* Lexington, MA: Lexington Books, 1982.
Sgroi, Suzanne, Linda Blick, and Francis Porter. "A Conceptual Framework for Child Sexual Abuse." In *Handbook of Clinical Intervention in Child Sexual Abuse*, Suzanne Sgroi, 9–38. Lexington, MA: Lexington Books, 1982.
Silver, Roxane L., Cheryl Boon, and Mary H. Stones. "Searching for Meaning in Misfortune: Making Sense of Incest." *Journal of Social Issues* 39 (1983): 81–102.
Sloan, Paul, and Eva Karpinsky. "Effects of Incest on the Participants." *American Journal of Orthopsychiatry* 12 (1942): 666–74.
Smith-Rosenberg, Carol. "The Female World of Love and Ritual." *Signs* 1 (1975): 1–30.
Spradley, James P. *The Ethnographic Interview.* NY: Holt, Rinehart and Winston, 1977.
Strauss, Patricia Lawrence. "A Study of the Recurrence of Father-Daughter Incest Across Generations." Ph.D. diss., California School of Professional Psychology, 1981.
Summit, Roland, and JoAnn Kryso. "Sexual Abuse of Children: A Clinical Spectrum." *American Journal of Orthopsychiatry* 48 (1978): 237–51.
Surrey, Janet L. "Mother-Blaming and Clinical Theory." In *Woman-Defined Motherhood*, Jane Price Knowles and Ellen Cole, eds., 83–87. Binghamton, NY: Harrington Park Press, 1991.
Szegedy-Maszak, Marianne. "Who's to Judge?" *New York Times Magazine*, May 21, 1989, 28.
Taubman, Stan. "Incest in Context." *Social Work* 28 (1984): 35–40.
"The Readers Write." *NASW News*, May 1984, 24.
Tierney, Kathleen J., and David L. Corwin. "Exploring Intrafamilial Child Sexual Abuse: A Systems Approach." In *The Dark Side of Families: Current Family Violence Research*, David Finkelhor, Richard Gelles, Gerald Hotaling, and Murray Straus, eds., 102–16. Beverly Hills, CA: Sage, 1983.
Tormes, Yvonne. *Child Victims of Incest.* Denver: Children's Division, The American Humane Association, 1968.
Truesdell, Donna L., John S. McNeil, and Jeanne P. Deschner. "Incidence of Wife Abuse in Incestuous Families." *Social Work* 31 (1986): 138–40.
Walker, Lenore E. *The Battered Woman.* NY: Harper and Row. Colophon Books, 1979.
Wardel, Laurie, Dair L. Gillespie, and Ann Leffler. "Science and Violence Against Wives." Department of Sociology, University of Utah, 1981. Unpublished manuscript.
Watson, Russel. "A Hidden Epidemic." *Newsweek*, May 14, 1984, 30.
Waterman, Jill. "Family Dynamics of Incest with Young children." In *Sexual Abuse of Children*, Kee MacFarlane and Jill Waterman, 204–219. NY: Guilford, 1986.
Wattenberg, Esther. "In a Different Light: A Feminist Perspective on the Role of Mothers in Father-Daughter Incest." *Child Welfare* LXIV (1985): 203–11.

Weber, Ellen. "Incest: Sexual Abuse Begins at Home." *Ms.*, April 1977, 64.

Weber, Max. *The Theory of Social and Economic Organization.* NY: Oxford University Press, 1947.

Weinberg, S. Kirson, *Incest Behavior.* Revised paperbound edition. NY: Citadel, 1976.

Weiner, Irving B. "Father-Daughter Incest." *Psychiatric Quarterly* 36 (1962): 607–32.

Westcott, Marcia. "Mothers and Daughters in the World of the Fathers." *Frontiers* 3 (1978): 16–21.

White, Leslie A. "The Definition and Prohibition of Incest." *American Anthropologist* 50 (1948): 416–35.

Woodbury, John, and Elroy Schwartz. *The Silent Sin.* NY: Signet, 1971.

Wrong, Dennis. "Some Problems Defining Social Power." *American Journal of Sociology* 73 (1968): 673–81.

Index

JANIS TYLER JOHNSON is Professor of Sociology and Social Work at Immaculata College. She has been a social worker in the fields of community mental health, family service, and public child welfare and has trained and consulted with professionals from different disciplines in the area of child sexual abuse.